The Identity Reset

The Identity Reset

A Guide to Discovering Yourself After Loss, Change, and Survival

Ashley Olivia Nelson

JOSSEY-BASS™
A Wiley Brand

Published by John Wiley & Sons, Inc., Hoboken, New Jersey.

ISBNs: 9781394337309 (Hardback), 9781394337323 (ePDF), 9781394337316 (ePub)

Library of Congress Control Number is Available

Cover Design: Paul McCarthy
Cover Art: © Getty Images | Labsas
Printed and bound by CPI Group (UK) Ltd, Croydon, CR0 4YY
C9781394337309_260126

To Devans Eli and Sharisse McClure—
Thank you for encouraging the
real me to show up.
And when she did,
being safe enough for her to stay.

To Stephenie de Hildegard—
You said if you didn't have bad luck,
you wouldn't have luck at all.
But maybe that's because
you gave your goodness away so freely,
you forgot to count it.
(I didn't.)

To my readers:
If you've never had someone see the
real you and stay—
may these pages be the beginning.

Contents

About the Author

Ashley Olivia Nelson is the founder of Learning About Grief, where she helps those experiencing loss and identity transitions. Since 2013, she has worked in grief across the healthcare, mental health, life insurance, and funeral care industries. Twice widowed, Ashley brings both professional insight and personal understanding to every conversation about loss and renewal. Her work has appeared in *POPSUGAR, Marie Claire, Shape,* and *Next Avenue*. Explore more of her work at ashleyolivianelson.com

Acknowledgments

Of My Builders and *Blessings*

For the voyage across the depth of who I am today, and as a byproduct, what this book has become, I have many to thank for steering me when I needed guidance, extending their presence to me, and helping me to make it safely on shore.

To my beloved late Jason and Michael, two loves lost sooner than I would have ever imagined. Thank you for seeing the raw truth of me—the messy, the ugly, the bold and courageous and kind. You witnessed my becoming with love and gentleness and challenged me where it was most needed. Your souls left my life, but never my story.

To my dearest of friends, you saw the "me" beneath the grief and the ambition. You reminded me of who I was when

I struggled to be her and celebrated the many versions that emerged. Thank you for being my builders and carrying my heart when I didn't know how to carry it myself. For your laughter, your grace, and friendship, thank you to Meghan Reale, Ruby Taylor, Bianca and Lawrence Ford, James Mackey, Drè Guy, and Annette Maturan. A special thank you to Erica Jeudy and Nicholle Caserta for your enduring friendship. To Claire Lucas, for your rare blend of honesty and love given in ways that are as uncommon as they are unforgettable. To Maria Tapas, I don't know how I would have survived endless hours of writing and living without you; thank you for being a champion of me. To Donovon FFriend, long before these pages existed, you said my lessons would make a book one day. Thank you for the consistent encouragement that helped carry this manuscript across the finish line.

To the mentors and healers in my life: You are witnesses of my becoming, steady as old trees, soft as new growth. There are never enough words I can offer to sing the praises of those who have helped, encouraged, and guided me along the way. Thank you to Natalie Huston, Deanna Danielian, Nikolai Chapochnikov, and Steve Roller for your compassion interwoven with creativity. I extend eternal gratitude to Noëlle Opsahl for helping me see *me*, and Leslie Lind-Hernaiz for being one of the biggest supporters of this book journey, all while tenderly helping me navigate the life I juggled in between.

To my MAAD ladies, Maki Iwase, Ann Veilleux, and Dana Cadonau-Huseby: Thank you for letting me be an "A" among the group. I smile every time I think of you. We started out as students learning IFS to help people heal, and years later, here we all are. How lucky am I to have trained with such an amazing group of therapists turned friends who I can rely upon for wisdom and love.

To my favorite last responders, the Fairchild family: Trish, Tony, Stephenie, Samantha, Arielyn, Douglas, Pat, Brendan, and so many others. Thank you for answering my deepest and most intricate questions about grief, death, and dying. Thank you for being a place of shared dark humor without apology—and infinitely so. Your immense sense of empathy, understanding, and knowledge has made an indelible difference in my life.

To the people who helped make this book great and carried its message: Thank you to my editor-friend Shalya Raquel, who helped me refine my book's outline years before I ever had a publisher. Thank you, Richelle Fredson, who after a brief conversation, encouraged me to write the proposal for this specific book idea. To the team at Wiley, thank you Amy Fandrei for believing in the message of this book, but also your patience. Thank you for reaching out to me again, and again (and again) to write this book. Thank you to my editors: Sophie Thompson, Christine O'Connor, Sunnye Collins, and Catherine Mallon. To Paul McCarthy for the beautiful book design: I shared what I didn't want it to look like because I didn't know what I wanted, and you created a design I adore.

To my team of wonderful professionals: my publicists, Danielle Wright and Dorianne Kaboya, for your creativity, and Beverly Beal, Esq. for ensuring I'm always protected; thank you to Andrea A. Moore for running my Grief Gatherings so I could step away to write. Thank you to Susan Trumpler, such a wonderful business coach you are, and among the first to encourage me to teach on identity. Thank you to Lise Bram for your excellence in outreach.

To the Learning About Grief community, thank you for entrusting to me the most vulnerable parts of your lives—your pain, your joy, your secrets that haven't felt safe elsewhere.

The greatest responsibility we have outside of ourselves is to steward one another well. I am grateful that out of all the places and people you could confide in, you chose me.

A heartfelt thank you to those who entrusted me with your stories during the research and interviews behind this book. Though your names remain unwritten, your insights, humanity, and remarkable courage are imprinted on these pages and held with honor.

To my clients—both past and present—you are one of my greatest gifts on this side of heaven. As I always tell you, I wish I had met you on the beach, sipping a cold glass of lemonade, but since hardship brought us together, I thank you with my whole heart for allowing me to not only be a part of your journey, but also to partake in the formation of your life with you.

To my family: Aaron, thank you for being a confidant, a protector, and a constant place of laughter. To Aliyah, for your moments of care and love. Thank you to my twin and her husband, Shakyra and Davon Winn, for your love and support; Auntie Glenda, who I called every forty-eight hours with a new book update, frustration, or milestone to celebrate; and my parents for their support along the journey. To Jason and Michael's family, thank you for sharing your heart with mine—and all these years later.

To my readers and all others unnamed: I know hope is possible because you exist. Thank you for the offering of your time and heart to listen, to read.

To my mentors and friends who didn't get to see this book come into fruition, but whose memory continues: Fred Griffin, Arthur Morrison, Umberto Perrone, Juaquan Taylor, Abronda Rich.

Author's Note

Throughout this book, in addition to changing names and altering identifying details, I've chosen to soften the sharper edges of certain stories—including my own and those that were generously entrusted to me. The stories told here are composites, and some of the more painful details have been intentionally left out—not to diminish their truth but to make it easier for your heart and mind to read through them.

While full, unfiltered stories can help us feel seen, they can also weigh heavily. They can anchor us in someone else's experience in a way that makes it harder to stay present with our own.

So, I made a conscious choice:

To keep the essence of each story's impact while removing the details that might make the journey feel too overwhelming. To help you feel understood, not overburdened. To create space for *your* reflection, not just someone else's pain.

Because this book isn't about other people's stories, it's about your relationship with your own, and who you're still becoming.

With kindness and intention,
—Ashley Olivia Nelson

Introduction

You don't expect to be widowed twice before you've turned thirty, but that's what happened to me. Unexpectedly, without warning or any idea of how or why, I found myself grieving on my grandmother's daybed, crying my soul out like I was auditioning for the most depressing soap opera ever. It felt like my tears were dripping with blood because the life I knew, the one I had imagined, was gone.

Loss has a way of doing that. It carves out parts of you, leaving questions, pain, and a hole where certainty once existed. And while that pain was crushing, I knew that death wasn't the only form of loss that would leave its mark.

Over a lifetime, you and I will experience many "deaths," be it a divorce, a romantic or friendship breakup, or a financial collapse. That's because grief is a shapeshifter: It emerges from people, places, and things, both seen and unseen. It lingers in the hearts of children who are neglected, abandoned, or fostered. It masks itself in addictions and in those who love the addicted—whether to drugs, work, food, or other habits we've deemed more acceptable. And let us not forget the immense loss of health following an unfavorable medical diagnosis.

These various losses can haunt us in different ways, but in that moment, grief wasn't hiding at all. It was sitting right next to me, fully present, in the shape of my soulmate's death. And as I lay there on the bed, consumed with the pain of a hundred grieving souls, Grandmother exhaled a long sigh from her favorite green chair. Her chin dropped to greet her heart, and the sadness of her soul met mine.

"I know the feeling," she said, her voice heavy with her own stories of grief. Then she rose, straightened her favorite blue-and-white house dress, and began gathering pillows from every corner of the room. We always joked that she must've bought all the pillows in the department store.

But before she got too far, she paused and looked at me with sad eyes. "Oh, my goodness! David died? My God!"

"No, Grandma," I said gently, stressing his name this time. "*Jason* died."

"Oh no, not David," she repeated, shaking her head as she stacked pillows around me like some sort of emotional fortress. "I can't believe it!"

My grandmother had dementia and often missed details, even in moments like this. I took my fingers and rubbed my temples, then stifled a chuckle. "Grandma, it's *Jason. Jason.*" She stared at me blankly, and all I could think was, *Jay, if you're listening, I promise she's talking about you.*

Yet, there was no convincing her. She started muttering to herself about all the things she knew about Jason—his kindness, how he gave me the most beautiful sunflowers, the stories our niece shared about him rolling down the car windows on summer days and singing country songs in their most terrible of voices. Her tales of him ran long—and yes, all while insisting his name was David. Despite the tears in my eyes, I couldn't help but laugh. Even in grief, there were moments like this—times that were both maddening and oddly comforting, where love and memory danced in harmony.

"Here's a blanket," she said finally, snapping me back into the present. Grandma tucked it around me as if I were a newborn in need of protection, smiled, and headed toward her chair.

But before she could sit, a relative entered the room and began interrogating me with questions I wasn't ready to answer. My mind couldn't compute. I felt more overwhelmed. It had only been a few hours since he had died, and already, people wanted details.

"Alright! That's enough now! You go," Grandma said, shooing them out of the room.

"But—but—but—" she didn't let them finish speaking. Mid-sentence, she grabbed the doorknob, gently pushed them out, and slammed the door with a finality only a grandma could get away with.

She turned around and looked at me. Her eyes were resolute. "Sometimes, you have to shut people out until you're ready," she said.

As she spoke, her words unlocked a memory I hadn't thought about in years, and my body became an iceberg I couldn't thaw. My mind drifted back to when I was nine years old, standing in my grandparents' kitchen. My entire family was there, but sometime that evening, Grandma and my parents slipped away and went out. When they returned, I jumped up with my arms open wide to embrace Grandma, but she walked by me without a wince of acknowledgment. It was as if she were in a trance, fixed on where she was going and oblivious to her normal surroundings. She moved throughout her home like a resident and a foreigner. Something was different about her. It was like all the warmth and tenderness she normally embraced escaped her.

"What happened?" I said to my aunt, who stood behind me.

She shrugged in confusion. "I'm not sure, Ash."

We watched Grandma walk out of her L-shaped dining room, through one kitchen door, and out the other, and down the long corridor. She hadn't even bothered to turn the lights on. Grandma went into her room and slammed the door. The house rumbled, then grew silent. It was like the heartbeat of her home had stopped. Years would go by before being in stillness felt safe again.

I remember the faint light peeking through the bottom of her door. I later learned that Grandpa had died at the hospital, and she didn't get a chance to say goodbye.

It's odd how I sensed it, maybe it was a subtle shift inside me, but something said that the grandma who walked inside that door would not be the same person who walked out. In a matter of minutes, everything changed, and I witnessed the first lesson loss would teach me: You don't just lose people—you lose parts of yourself, too.

Gradually, the memory faded, and the present day me took over. I could feel the pillows around me as the sights and sounds of the moment came into my awareness. But then, as I frantically looked around the room, I realized something chilling: *Now I was the one behind the door.* Grief had isolated and reshaped me. Who would I become when I walked out?

The Identity Arc

That question lingered in my soul. It hummed like the last note trembling in the air long after the choir had stopped singing. I'd felt life's bruises before, but none of them uprooted me. This time was different. I felt like a tree, innocently caught by the winds and rains of a storm. I had toppled over, and my roots were showing. Each one held secrets, stories, family lineage, joys and sorrows, moments I had felt but didn't have names and language for. I questioned why every time I tried to get up, something else would unravel. Then I realized—you can't repot a plant without each of its roots feeling the motion.

Your life feels tender, raw, and exposed. Truths you thought you had buried resurrect themselves. Your roots, tilted by the hurricane of life, long to be touched and seen. But when they are, you uncover aspects of yourself you never knew existed.

From the moment you were born, your foundation began forming long before you ever had a say. Your name was chosen before you understood what it meant. You were dressed in clothes that signaled your gender, born into a family whose status and story became part of yours. The environment you were raised in—the voices, the patterns, the air of a home—shaped your temperament and quirks, all without your permission.

Maybe you were calm and called "a good baby," the kind that made life easier for everyone else. Or you were louder, more curious, and heard words like "busy body" or "too much." From the very start, people around you attached meaning to who you were—sometimes praising it, sometimes correcting it. So, it's no wonder that when someone says, "Tell me about yourself," you're inclined to answer with roles, failures, and successes. What if all of it—labels, shame, accolades, and failures—were stripped away? Who would you be if no one was left to tell you who you are?

That question is where my journey began too. Long before Jason died, I was already working in grief—helping families and having conversations about their death losses and major life transitions. Over the years, that support deepened as I became an IFS-informed practitioner, someone who's been trained and supervised in a psychotherapeutic, evidence-based model that helps people understand the inner patterns and protective instincts that shape their psychological world. My life's work has led me through nearly every layer of the grief and death care ecosystem. I've answered the calls at a funeral home that begin with, "They were just pronounced," and helped push caskets down quiet hallways. I've watched firsthand how grief brings out both the best and the hardest parts of our humanity.

I've sat in insurance offices where loss had to be spoken of in numbers, and in board meetings with mental-health researchers still searching for language that could hold pain. Beyond those spaces, I've led grief support groups, facilitated identity sessions, and sat across from people whose losses didn't begin with death but instead divorce, infertility, career changes, and empty-nesting. People whose endings came too soon and whose beginnings arrived too late.

Through it all, one truth has held: Neither grief nor identity end at the point of change; it continues to evolve long after the world expects closure and reshapes the person who survives. Today, this insight shapes how I write, teach, and support others in the work of building identity across every part of life—personal, professional, and collective. For each story I've witnessed carries the same thread: When life rearranges us, our identity asks to be transformed.

Life is strange like that. Sometimes, you don't realize you've been knocked down until you're looking at a sky you don't recognize. And so, as I gathered each tangled strand of my story, I noticed a pattern. I first began testing it out on my life, then shared it with friends and trusted people. Over and over, the positive results yielded the same. People found courage, healing, clarity, and lived versions of themselves they dreamed of having. Now, I share it with my clients, and for the first time—*you*.

The Five Roots

Each person has five roots that get exposed after a loss, life transition, or tragedy, and each reveals a piece of who we are and how we cope. Regardless of the age or trauma, where you live, the money you have, the person you are, these roots exist. You and I will talk about each of these roots because it's important you know them. While we go deeper into each root throughout our time together, here's an introduction. Consider if any of them have appeared in your life. You can view it as cracking a mystery, where you are a detective and the gold you find is yours.

Root 1: The Shapeshifter (Chapters 1–3)

This root digs itself inward to help you adapt, protect, and endure. It takes on the burden of supporting you through your day-to-day realities: putting on a good face at work when chaos awaits at home, being the parent who can maintain a routine after their second-born died, and the one holding onto friendships. It carries the weight of survival. Shapeshifting is clever armor. It disguises, shelters, and buys time. It can also cling so tightly that you start mistaking the mask as you. When the disguises fall away, the harder questions begin to whisper and that leads us to the next root.

Root 2: The Truth Seeker (Chapters 4–6)

Have you asked yourself, "Why now?" or "What really happened?" This is the root that gives you clarity and learns to discern what's honest. It teaches you how to trust yourself and, if you're willing, to trust others too. The Truth Seeker makes room for curiosity and presence—especially when life becomes disruptive.

Root 3: The Releaser (Chapters 7–8)

The heart often clings to what was never meant to be carried. We arrive here tangled in stories and expectations—some chosen, many inherited. This root teaches us the art of loosening our grip. The release comes as we set down guilt, self-criticism, shame, and the grief we mistook for responsibility. In that surrender, exhaustion lightens, breath returns, and life can root again.

Root 4: The Builder (Chapters 9–11)

Ironically, in the aftermath of almost anything, aspects of what was remain. It's the one tree that didn't burn during the fire. Uncle's favorite cap that survived the flood. The hope to make it through another day, or the laughter that emerges between tears. Release creates space, but space alone doesn't rebuild a life. Once you've let go, you must decide how to live differently—and how to show that difference to others. The Builder Root is about expression. It teaches you how to step into your renewed identity in practical ways, how to communicate your truth with consistency, and the three kinds of relationships you need to expand your capacity as you grow into wholeness.

Root 5: The Identity Root (Chapters 12–13)

The Identity Root isn't about going back to who you were; it's about engaging with an essence you may have never fully known. Here, identity becomes less of a label and more of a lived presence—an artwork made of layers, cracks, colors, and textures that reflects the fullness of who you are. One of its greatest gifts is peace: the assurance that you no longer have to perform, prove, or pretend to belong, succeed, or thrive. You are free to be safe with yourself and with others. The Identity Root becomes a compassionate guide that's capable of shifting through the rubble of life while keeping you secure in a deeper purpose above ground.

You've Worked Hard Enough

These roots aren't a step-by-step guide or a one-size-fits-all solution. They are markers of the internal terrain we navigate after loss—reminders that the person you are becoming is shaped not just by *what* you've endured, but *how* you've endured it. You might already suspect which of the five roots resonates with you—or maybe you see pieces of each winding throughout your story. Either way, understand that what lies ahead isn't about "fixing" yourself; it's about being seen, held, and understood.

When a soldier gets injured, we don't say they fought poorly or that they are broken. We don't get angry at them for having "lost" a battle either. We say they are courageous and got wounded in the process of survival. *Remember: We fix broken things, but we care for wounded people.* Your woundedness does not make you broken. It makes you audacious. Now, it's time for you to be taken care of.

Yet, being on the receiving side of care might feel foreign, uncomfortable, or unnecessary. After forging the trials of life solo, it can be easy to grow accustomed to doing things alone. That's normal and expected. You've put in a lot of work to get this far, more than anyone has likely acknowledged. You've fought silent battles, and if you're someone who's used to being "the strong one," and "holding it all together," or "never letting anyone see you cry, bend, or break," then allowing tender parts of you to be touched might feel threatening. Exposing a wound can be risky. *How do I know if I can trust you?* It might create a knee-jerk reaction of anger, sadness, and skepticism. That's okay. I welcome them. Really, I do. They don't scare me. Your body is saying, *This is different. We're not used to this. Stay back or give me a minute!* That's healthy. And although I know it's safe, I want you to feel safe too. Take this journey as slowly as you need.

For now, it's okay to honor a gentle process or one that feels uncomfortable. It's normal to sense a push-pull dynamic of wanting to trust the process yet doubting it too. When change happens, intuition and fear become twin voices that whisper in the same ear—one is a true guiding conscience, and the other keeps in mind past hurts and pains. Both want the same thing: for you to be protected and prevent reinjury. As you explore the Identity Arc in your own life, you'll gain discernment on how to distinguish those voices.

Please know that this guide to your internal terrain has intentional pitstops: those of empathy and compassion, and small, easy-to-apply actions to decrease the overwhelm in your life. You don't have to work so hard when your roots are untangled and planted upright. So, for now, take a breath: inhale, exhale. Feel welcome to reread that sentence as many times as you need. (I do it often.) Let these words be the instrument that carry peace to your mind, a nurturing presence to your heart, and guidance to your soul.

Root One

THE SHAPESHIFTER

Chapter 1

It's Not All About Death

We think of grief as losing a person, but what about losing who we were? Losing a role, a purpose, a version of ourselves that felt certain and stable? That's grief too—one that doesn't come with a clear path forward. It's true that, culturally, we don't know what to say or do when someone dies. How much harder is it to eulogize a living person, especially when that person is the former "you"? The loss of identity is rarely talked about but impacts nearly every aspect of your life. Some people bury the tension that arrives around this. Others face it head-on. Regardless, it's one of the most destabilizing forms of grief, and it makes you question everything:

> Who am I without this person, this role, this life I built?
> If I'm not that person anymore, what's left of me?
> Do I even recognize myself? Do others?

Loss isn't confined to sadness—it shifts into disorientation. Most times, you can never emotionally prepare for it. Loss shows up like an unexpected houseguest who messes up your plans and eats up all your energy. One day, you're fine, and the next, grief is lounging on your couch, reminding you of all the places it's been. You look around, trying to figure out what it took and, worse, what it left behind. As the years pass, you wake up one day, wondering why you're not where you thought you'd be and feeling disappointed with how life turned out.

We don't talk about this enough. We've limited grief to being about the death of a person, but what about all the other stuff that dies? There's no funeral for your self-esteem after a toxic relationship. No flowers laid down for the investments you've lost. No bagpipes playing for the sacrifices you've made. Imagine if there were, though! "Here lies Tina's patience, survived by three unanswered texts and the sympathy casserole no one actually ate." As much as we try to laugh it off—and believe me, I have tried *and* failed—there's always that feeling that nothing is the same.

Two Childhoods, One Grief

I first realized this as a kid when my childhood friend, Marilyn, moved away. She and I were inseparable. From hopscotch to hula-hoop, jump rope, and freeze tag, we knew how to have fun. Whenever we weren't playing, we'd sit on the concrete stoop to talk about things adults felt we weren't supposed to know, or we didn't feel safe telling them.

"I wish I had a different family," I said to Marilyn, looking at the street.

"Why? You're lucky," she said with her face scrunched up.

I sighed. *Lucky* was a word I was used to hearing. From the outside, people looked at me like I lived in a sitcom with a happy ending. I lived with my parents, had siblings, and grew up in a house. But what happened inside that house wasn't so lucky, and I didn't know how to explain that. I saw Marilyn's parents, who seemed attentive, happy to have her, and generally pleasant. In contrast, I didn't feel loved or noticed by mine.

"Do you ever wish you were adopted?" I asked her.

"I *am* adopted. I don't know who my real mom and dad are," she said with her head down. I watched as she traced imaginary figures on the concrete with her finger. "I guess they didn't want me."

It seemed strange. We were two kids, in completely different situations, and yet, we both felt unwanted. That moment stuck with me. It taught me that grief isn't limited to what was lost—it's also shaped by what was never given yet deeply longed for. And as sad as it was, it felt good to say it out loud. I wasn't alone in the pain and longing, which meant a lot as a kid because I didn't have many safe places.

A few weeks after that conversation, Marilyn came over and said she was moving to a different part of the country. The idea of her leaving eclipsed my soul. *Who would I share my feelings with? Who would laugh alongside me? Now I won't have a friend.* I didn't have playdates. My classmates didn't come to my house, and I didn't go to theirs. When Marilyn moved, the only company I had would disappear. It made me question where I belonged. Who was I without her? If my safe person was gone, did I still matter?

Dread hit me hard as I counted the days until Marilyn would leave me, and in the meantime, whatever fun we had or stories we shared, I tried soaking it up. But time moves unevenly in grief. One moment you feel frozen, and the next, it speeds by like the ten-minute snooze button on your alarm. It just . . . *goes.*

I still remember the day Marilyn moved. She came over and walked to the door with slumped shoulders and a long face. We both knew what the moment meant, and neither of us was ready for it. I don't think we're ever ready for loss—even when we see it coming.

Marilyn gave me a long hug and waved goodbye as she walked toward the moving van. I felt a mix of anger, sadness, and helplessness. How could someone I trusted and cared about be taken this easily? I watched the car pull off until I couldn't see it anymore, and that was it. No calls, no letters, just silence. Our friendship was over. Marilyn and I never spoke again.

I told the adults around me, "It stinks that she moved," and they responded, "Yeah, that happens sometimes. Parents decide to leave." But they didn't get it. Her moving wasn't a simple change of address; it was losing companionship, shared jokes, and having a friend I could reach over the fence and hug.

With no other kids my age on the block, I felt lonely. I went into my backyard and thought about the times she and I would chat about dolls, the animals we liked, or winter recess. I didn't have language for it then, so the loneliness deepened. Grief can do that—make the world feel bigger and you feel smaller. The more time passed, the more I felt was taken from me because of her absence.

Can I Grieve That?

Have you ever felt a single loss unravel so many threads in your life? One loss ripples into countless others. Psychologists call these secondary losses. I call it grief's encore performance. After the initial event, there's another right behind it with a similar intensity. For example, the main event might be a job loss. Then other losses that follow—the kids stopping dance lessons, not being able to afford a vacation, having to purchase foods that aren't as healthy, not making the rent, losing your health insurance—are all secondary losses. Aspects of life that were once normal, perhaps needed, have been stripped from you.

Maybe it's the death of a loved one. A parent dies, and now you're grieving them not being present at a milestone event or meeting their grandchild. A spouse dies, and you're left without your chief encourager, and the person who was the only family you could rely upon or who you dreamed of building a family with. Your sibling dies, and the memory keeper of family jokes, the one who shared responsibilities of checking in on your parents—or complaining about them with you—is now gone. Even losses such as divorces, health setbacks, a pet dying, or a car being totaled disrupt the dynamics of *life as you knew it*. No one tells you that. Instead, they say, "Be strong," as if carrying emotional weight is the equivalent to strength conditioning at the gym. One loss begetting another is not the obstacle course you willingly signed up for.

As a grief specialist, I've had more than a handful of clients who were grieving the end of a long-term relationship, or one that they thought was promising. They lost not only a partner, but their sense of security, their social circle, and their confidence. It took months for them to realize that grieving these smaller losses was as important as grieving the big one.

Perhaps you've felt grief too, be it a friendship breakup, having your trust betrayed, losing the freedom of working at home or in the office—whichever was your preference. From family estrangement to loss of physical mobility—the list of what we grieve feels endless. These are the kinds of losses that people brush off as "life," even when they reorder everything you rely on. You don't need tragedy to feel undone; sometimes the smallest shifts are the ones that hit the hardest.

Loss Is a Full-Body Experience

When loss has shaken up your life, slowing down and stepping back can be helpful. You might find yourself struggling to eat or consuming more than normal. Perhaps your sleep habits have changed: restless, you toss and turn, your endless thoughts and silent tears and frustrations keep you awake, or stuck in bed. Going to work or school feels harder. You struggle to concentrate. The tasks you're great at grow in difficulty. What you've never had to think about, you suddenly forget. *What's happening to me?* Anxiety and stress start to build up. You feel frustrated that you don't have the capacity to do what you once did.

You wonder why you're slacking off, resting too much, or drifting from your personal standards. When physical changes begin to happen, the tension within us increases. Some people bury themselves in work, scrolling, recreational drugs, binge-watching TV, their art, whatever seems convenient and pleasurable. As your energy decreases and pulls in new directions, it's easy to question what's happening and why.

Grief likes to be in the limelight. It speaks in whatever way it thinks it can grab your attention. Dr. Joe Dispenza, a researcher in neuroscience, quantum physics, and epigenetics, wrote in his book, *You Are the Placebo: Making Your Mind Matter*, "As thoughts are the language of the brain, feelings are the language of the body." These reactions aren't signs of weakness; they're natural responses to profound changes in your life. If you've experienced these things, you're not alone. It's more common than you think.

Loss is universal—it touches the rich and poor, people of every race and nation, and scientists have done studies that show various animal species grieve, too. Unfortunately, grief goes unseen because we don't recognize it within the human collective. What if we made room for all forms of grief and acknowledged every loss that impacts us as important? Maybe we'd feel more supported and better understood when death happens.

If you've ever experienced the death of a loved one (or pet), you might have felt the heart-shattering pain that follows. Some moments we think to ourselves, "Is this real? I can't believe they're gone. Did they ever exist?" You wonder if you've made it all up. The emotional turmoil within you goes unnoticed as everyone else's life goes on. They continue working at their jobs while you're grieving an ending of your own. They return home to their families with everyone at the table, while the one you loved is dead and gone.

The empty chair at dinner leaves a harsh reminder. When the sentimental item you had breaks or gets stolen, when the pieces of your heart feel gone with the person who died, as the relationship you poured everything into crumbles into something irreparable, grief shows up.

Grief often feels too big to share, too heavy to carry, and too overwhelming to put into words.

Your dreams are the hopeful, unachievable bliss you wish you had, and your life becomes the inescapable nightmare.

This Will Be the Death of Me

Growing up, whenever we did a magic trick, we'd say: "Abracadabra. Now you see it. Now you don't." Well, you can think of loss the same way: "Now you have it. Now you don't." Except when it comes to the fabric of who you and I are, it's about who we *were* versus who we are *now*. The devoted caregiver who suddenly has no one else to care for. The athlete who spent decades training, only to retire and ask, "What now?"

We come to understand that the whirlwind of thoughts and emotions of life's most anticipated and happy moments are tainted with loss. Graduations, promotions, and leaving one neighborhood for another are no exception. Journalist Ron Riddell wrote about sending his children off to college. He said, "My wife [described] a dagger of pain in the grocery store when she bought a packet of brown paper lunch bags for the last time," and "parents have told me to expect a multitude of emotions, but surely the most immediate will be the sense of loss in the weeks after departure."[1] These milestones carry gain and grief in the same breath, revealing how loss threads itself into moments we assume should feel uncomplicated.

However, these changes expand beyond home and family. As technology advances, we might foresee a day when entire careers—or segments of industries—become obsolete. This will impact those who aspired to fulfill these roles, or whose lives were deeply molded around them. So, when

[1] Ron Riddell, "Now That My Kids Are Off to College, What's This Empty Nester Dad to Do?" CNN, August 23, 2025, https://www.cnn.com/2025/08/10/health/empty-nester-parents-wellness

you think of the ways you've lost yourself, or the ways you've witnessed others lose aspects of who they were, what comes to mind?

Before Loss	**After Loss**
I knew my role in life.	I don't know my purpose anymore.
I felt secure in my relationships.	What's wrong with me? I feel abandoned.
I had a clear vision for my future.	I can barely plan for the next day or months.
I recognized myself.	I'm not sure who I am.
I had trust in the world and confidence.	Life feels uncertain and I second-guess myself.

When your identity shatters, what felt secure and safe gets replaced with anxiety and doubt. You sit in the wreckage of what was, hoping to recognize something—*anything*—that still belongs to you. Questions arrive, and many don't have an immediate answer. It all gets muddled together. It's normal not to have it "all figured out." You start questioning everything—your past, your future, and that tattoo you got at nineteen. You wonder if you're overreacting or if most people are better at pretending than you are. Spoiler alert: they are. Cheers to you for being bold enough to show it. While loss rips up what you once thought permanent, and that's terrifying, it also gives you room to decide what happens next, not in a "bounce back and be stronger" and "you're resilient" kind of way—ugh, *no*—but in a quiet, human way. Trust me, you don't have to rush to rebuild. Breathe long enough to notice—*you're still here*. Maybe, just maybe, *here* is where you get to meet the person you're becoming through this.

Friendly Recap

- Loss isn't limited to death; it appears in the roles we outgrow, the identities we shed, and the versions of ourselves we can no longer return to.
- The emotional, physical, and relational fallout of loss is real—your body and mind respond to change long before you have language for it.
- Every transition leaves an imprint. Which loss, change, or life shift has shaped who you've become today?

Chapter 2

It's Not Safe to Be Me

We don't strip naked in public for the same reason we don't strip off our emotional masks—we're ashamed. Vulnerability feels dangerous. Showing our true selves feels like standing exposed on the street—too much, too open, too raw.

As I told my childhood friend Marilyn, I often wished I had a different family—one where I'd never have to question if I was loved or "good enough." Over time, I realized wishing alone couldn't change that. So I did what many children in difficult homes do: I adapted. I tried refashioning myself into someone who might blend in and feel less neglected or, at least, not get pulled into the mental war zone. If I could be quieter and more agreeable, I'd escape the yelling, the in-home bullying with physical threats, and the disparaging remarks followed by, "I was only joking; you're too sensitive."

Making myself small became a skill I relied upon, and its rewards felt far greater than the foreseeable risks, for this wasn't a tactic; it was emotional survival. Perhaps, in your way, you've done something similar. Maybe you learned to silence your needs, ask for nothing, and want nothing—believing that doing so would keep you safe. Or you adopted the role of the tireless caretaker: the one who absorbs everyone else's burdens to avoid potential conflict. *If I make them happy, they won't leave.* You pour yourself out for others, even as your wishes are tucked away. You hope that the accolades and success you've built up won't reveal the pain you've pushed down.

These ways of living aren't flaws or indications that something is "wrong with you"—they show wisdom: when you had no other choice, you adapted. Nature is also a shapeshifter. A chameleon changes its colors according to its environment, and its ability to do so is more than instinct—it's science. Its skin contains nanocrystals that shift their position according to what the lizard needs to survive. The nanocrystals become tightly packed to reflect cooler colors like blue and green, or loosen to show warmer tones like yellow and red. The result? Shapeshifting. The chameleon reflects its surroundings perfectly—whether to blend in, stand out, or stay out of harm's way. I wonder what conditions you had to mirror when it wasn't safe to be yourself? How many of those cover-ups still shape you today, even when the danger has passed?

The mask starts as protection—but eventually, it becomes your face. If you learned that being quiet kept you safe, you stopped speaking up. If you learned that being easygoing kept you included, you stopped asking for what you needed. If you learned that fixing problems made you valuable, you became the fixer. And maybe now. . .you don't know how to stop.

> ***Our Survival Identity*** *isn't who we truly are; it's who we needed to become to endure life's chaos.*

Unfortunately, over time, we forget where the performance ends and we begin. Have you ever heard someone say, "I've always been this way. This is just how I am"? Maybe you've said it yourself. I know I have.

Yet, we may have relied on morphing our identity for so long, it becomes the only one we know. What's harder is that these roles often lead to praise from others, and that applause makes the acting role harder to quit.

I remember starting a new job, and a coworker said, "Let's introduce you to Stacey. If no one else knows how to handle something, Stacey knows, and if she doesn't know, well, we're all screwed." This approval is gratifying; it's proof that you're needed, valued, and indispensable. Because when the applause fades, when your performance is done and you're left alone with the exhaustion, the creeping realization hits: Who's going to take care of *me*?

If you've ever found yourself burned out by your role—be it as a quiet peacemaker, the "therapist" friend, or a self-reliant lone wolf—you're not alone. Still, we can come to understand that our masks were never meant to become part of our permanent identity. Yet, these realizations don't come easy. They often arise after hardship—when life's ordinary rhythms are disrupted by absence, upheaval, tragedy, or loss. Generally, the experiences that take us by surprise shake us the hardest. We're taught to plan for success, for a future family, a strong financial future, and the like. Rarely do we envision hardship in our dreams and how much it will impact us mentally and emotionally.

So, you might resist wearing all your different hats when life gets rough. The actions you once took to survive have become the behaviors that further deplete you. A longing for friends and family to step up stirs your soul. You want a break from it all. So, little by little, you begin to withdraw. Does someone want advice? *Nope. I'm not being the go-to listener.* Does your employer want someone to pick up the slack? *I'm not doing it. It'll get done tomorrow.* Does your family want you to put up with the same crap as always? *That's a hard pass for me.* Saying yes to what you'd normally allow gets tougher. Though you might struggle to set boundaries, having them becomes attractive.

Yet, stopping these habits isn't as easy as it seems. These traits don't feel inseparable from who you are. If I tell people no, does that mean I'm selfish? What if I disappoint my friends by not helping? My boss might think I'm unreliable if I call in for a day off. And if I tell the kids, "Mommy or Daddy needs a moment alone," am I failing as a parent? These thoughts linger for a reason. They're not just excuses; they're the echoes of the expectations you've shouldered. It's no wonder you sometimes feel trapped between what you've always done and what you desperately need.

The default response is to protect the fragile parts of ourselves. Hiding feels easier than risking rejection. Building walls is better than being vulnerable. Going numb means not feeling pain at all. Like me, you likely have good reasons for doing this. Maybe you were betrayed too many times and decided being open doesn't work. Or you saw others get hurt and promised yourself, *that won't be me.* Regardless of how you got here, it makes sense.

Our brains don't prioritize our happiness—they focus on keeping us going. If wearing a mask or hiding behind walls has felt like the only way to get you through, your mind will do that. Yet, here's the thing: the same patterns that helped you escape turmoil can also leave you feeling stuck. The question isn't just, "How do I survive?" anymore. It's "How do I truly live?"

For many of us, after a loss, letting go of more stuff—expectations, who we've known ourselves to be, relationships, or habits—feels too dangerous. It's yet another loss on top of having so much taken from you. To add to it, people might have realized you aren't the same person anymore, and perhaps you have too. You see yourself in old pictures, and who you were then seems like a stranger of the past, an existence you had lifetimes ago. You wonder how you got here and what the heck happened. How did I land in such misfortune?

While you might have accepted that you won't ever be that person again, friends and family wait on the sidelines for that version of you to reappear. No matter how much you've explained it to them, words fall short. They don't get it. Those who don't push you to return to your former self demand that you "move on" and "keep the past in the past," as if the pain and suffering aren't an integrated piece of who you are *now*. It's confusing. How can others not see it?

People See External Wounds—Not the Ones Inside

We live in a world that's quick to see everything except for a broken spirit. Society is adept at seeing what you should and shouldn't do, who you shouldn't and shouldn't be, and what it deems you should and shouldn't be achieving by now. But recognizing your grief? Seeing that you need a little more patience, love, and tenderness? Recognizing you're having a bad day? That seems beyond its ability.

While physical wounds require sight, internal wounds require in*sight.*

Of course, not seeing someone's internal wounds doesn't mean they don't exist. It can mean their invisibility invites people to discount your discomfort as insignificant.

If you've said, "see my heart" in a conversation, chances are, you were asking for this exact type of understanding. Through years of speaking with grieving hearts and those who self-identify with trauma, I've observed three primary reasons internal wounds aren't noticed by family, friends, and, perhaps, our medical professionals too:

1. **You appear to be "fine" on the outside.** People often assume your pain can't be *that* bad because you look composed, or you've tucked away what hurts. Remember, it's hard to find what we're not looking for, especially if it's intentionally lingering in the shadows.
2. **You minimize your own needs before anyone else gets the chance.** When others repeatedly miss or dismiss your internal pain, it makes sense that you'd start to do the same. Minimizing your own needs isn't a flaw—it's an adaptation. A quiet way of saying, I don't want to make things worse. Or, I've learned that being honest doesn't always make me safer.

   So you might find yourself smiling when you want to scream. Or saying, "It's not a big deal" when it is. You clean up your pain before anyone sees it, not because you're trying to hide—but because somewhere along the line, you learned it wasn't welcome.

   This isn't self-betrayal. It's self-protection. It's brilliant, for the purposes you developed this habit. It's not a fault or "problem" that you have. However, embracing your identity asks you to gently question if this once necessary strategy is still giving you the outcome you want. Is it keeping you safe—or contributing to you remaining unseen? (We'll talk about how to overcome this in future chapters.)

3. **Your pain might stir feelings family and friends have worked hard to avoid.** If yawning is contagious, then second to it are emotions. Have you ever passed by a stranger who smiled at you and you returned a smile? Or seen someone crying on the news and felt sad? And I think many of us have met someone whose laugh is funnier than the joke. I remember sitting on a train during rush hour and one man burst into laughter. My friends and I all started cracking up, as did those around us. One person yelled out, "Hey, man, are you serious? Is that really how you laugh?" The man laughed again and in second, the busy train roared with humor. Likewise, your vulnerability might nudge those around you to confront aspects of themselves they prefer to leave unseen. Truth works like a lamp—revealing what's hidden—and like salt in its oldest sense: cleansing what's tender and preserving what's valuable. When your honesty lights a room, it awakens what's within people and that can be jarring for them.

It's like having someone turn on the light while you're sleeping at 3 a.m. The brightness feels overpowering, and it takes time for your sight to adapt. This makes sympathy easier than empathy. Sympathy says, "I'm sorry that happened to you." Empathy says, "I am imagining myself in your shoes, and feeling your pain, and when I do, the wounds that you're experiencing feel heavy. It makes sense why you need time to do nothing; moments that give much and demand little; and why your capacity has changed." Dr. Frank Anderson gave the most beautiful expression of empathy: "I'm feeling my feelings while you're feeling your feelings."[1]

I remember grieving the loss of my soulmate and being told, "Pain builds character. Consider yourself lucky." Maybe that's true, but I was never asked if I already had too much pain, or if I already had enough character, *thank you very much.* As far as I was concerned, "luck," by their definition, was birthed out of pure heartache—which seemed, well, *unlucky.* When you've gone through enough distress to fill a library of therapy sessions, it's easy to believe suffering is in your DNA and, thereby, the only thing you can produce.

Struggle followed by struggle, disappointment after disappointment, it's amazing we get up and try again. Because when life takes a sharp turn, we don't just lose people we love or the things we've worked so hard to build. We also lose something even more personal: the story we've told ourselves about who we are. Maybe you thought of yourself as strong, dependable, or someone who always bounces back. Grief rewrites those narratives, and that's confusing. *If I'm not the person I was, and I can't be who others expect me to be, then who am I?*

The thing about pain is that it's sneaky. It doesn't knock before it enters, doesn't apologize for the mess it makes, and it certainly doesn't clean up after itself. Yet you don't become suspicious of it because the entire time, it's whispering, "Now that I'm here, you have a best friend." It doesn't tell you the hefty price tag it brings: isolation. They say, "misery loves company," but the truth is, misery loves confinement. Its shackles don't keep danger out—they keep you locked in.

---

[1] Anderson, F. (n.d.). *New Dimensions of Trauma Healing with Frank Anderson, MD.* Boulder, CO: Therapy Wisdom.

Misery wants you to believe you're the only one who feels this way and that no one else could possibly understand. Add grief to the mix, and suddenly, you've got enough emotional cocktails to keep you mentally hungover for years. It makes perfect sense why healing from anything—grief, trauma, or loss—takes so much longer than we ever imagined. If chaos is messy, cleaning up its aftermath is no less daunting. And what makes it harder is that this cleanup often feels like a solo job.

The people around you offer platitudes that don't fit what you're feeling. They tell you, "Whatever you're going through, you'll get through this." *Ok, but how? Can you help me to the other side?* Or my personal gripe: "Time heals all wounds." No, it doesn't. Time doesn't heal wounds—what we do with time does, and our life might not return to how it once was. We heal what can be healed, mend what can be mended, and carry what remains. Take a deep breath with me, will you? Inhale. Exhale.

Eventually, the fog begins to lift, and reality sets in, leaving you with a question: Do I stay chained, or do I risk setting myself free? On the surface, it might seem like an obvious choice. Who wouldn't want freedom? You and I both know that some things are easier said than done. Walking away from the weight of everything may feel uncertain and undesirable.

Why Losing Ourselves Feels Unsafe

When I was younger, I received one of my first lessons in shapeshifting. I withheld parts of the truth (which I later spent my early twenties correcting). I remember being a kid and getting reprimanded for small things.

One time, my aunt called to speak to my father, and as she waited for him to come to the phone, she asked me, "Oh, how's your mom doing?"

I was seven, so I told the truth. "She's feeling sick. She has a cold. I think she's lying down."

That seems like a typical, fair response. It was honest and didn't reveal much. But for my mother, who overheard it, it was worth getting enraged over. My mom ran out the room next to me, snatched the phone from my hand, and said to my aunt, "If you want to know how I'm doing, ask me. Don't ask my child!" She slammed the phone onto the receiver and then looked at me.

"Don't you ever—" she yelled, her finger pointing inches from my face, "tell anyone I am sick or not feeling well. And I AM *NOT* SICK! I'm tired!"

I peered over, seeing the crumpled tissues in her other hand, the cough medicine bottle on the green-tiled kitchen table, and the yellow lozenge bag nearby. Her sneezes broke the silence.

"But I thought you were sick," I said, trying to soften the fact of what I knew. "She only asked how you were; that's it. What was I supposed to say?"

"You're not listening to me! Do not tell anyone how I am doing," she moved her finger closer. "If I catch you answering any way other than 'ask my mom how she's doing' when they ask you, I'm beating your a-double-s. Do you understand me?"

My mom considered herself a devout religious person who never cursed. Apparently, spelling out "ass" as a-double-s didn't count. Terrified and confused, I nodded.

"Say it with your mouth," she yelled again, spit flying onto my face.

"Yes, I understand."

She walked away, stomped her feet with every step, grabbed the cough drops from the kitchen table and returned to the other room.

The Identity I Wanted

Never punish people for telling the truth. That's what I should have learned, but I didn't. Instead, there were many events where the lie was rewarded, and I spent the latter part of my teens trying not to associate honesty with harm.

I wanted to be someone who could be trusted—if I said it, people would know I meant it—whose actions aligned with my words, and there were no false stories to remember. When I took the mask off when I was alone, I'd journal all the real facts about what happened. Not just about me, but about whom I had to cover for. It was my way of upholding the truth privately, when it wasn't safe to do so publicly. Thankfully, adulthood freed me.

Yet that was also the scary part: Was it truly permissible to *be* that person? To become "better," or at least, more supportive of myself and others? I questioned it.

What if I show up as myself and it's not enough, or worse, too much?
What if I take the mask off and I'm rejected for it?
What if this version of me doesn't make it?

Looking back now, I realize this: *we know how to survive.* That's how you got this far. Survival—people-pleasing, shutting down or getting aggressive, twisting into someone more acceptable—is second nature. You were doing it before you realized. But survival isn't the same as living. And that's where things get uncomfortable because our identity is often tied to promises we've made long ago.

Friendly Recap

- The parts of you that learned to stay small, agreeable, or invulnerable weren't flaws—they were survival strategies built in unsafe or unpredictable environments.
- Masks form for protection, but over time they can blur into identity. Healing asks you to notice where the performance ends and where you begin.
- Every adaptation has a story behind it. Which role, mask, or learned behavior still shapes who you are today—and are you ready to explore who you might be without it?

Chapter 3

The Unspoken Agreements We Make with Pain

Never again. Two powerful words that are uttered after we have experienced life-changing events, betrayal, and loss.

"Never again" is the heart's outcry that *you don't get to do this to me anymore.* It's what we say when the hurt reaches the bones. I've heard friends say "never again" to re-partnering after being widowed (and understandably so). I've witnessed protest movements screaming "never again!" after someone was unjustly murdered. From clients to coworkers and strangers alike, "never again" shows up after bad business deals, a friend dishonors the other, or someone's heart has become collateral damage in the hands of a person they loved.

It's not a phrase—it's a vow. And let me tell you, "never again" doesn't always come out in a big, dramatic speech.

Sometimes it's a quiet, *man, I'm done,* or you cursing in the car, and blocking their number. People make these vows often. They sound like:

- "I won't let anyone see me cry."
- "If I don't expect anything, I can't be let down."
- "Everyone leaves eventually."

What you don't realize is that those "nevers" turn into policies. Like an airport security agent, you start scanning every feeling and gesture to see if it's carrying danger. Experience made you wiser, but it wounded you too. Some of what we call personality traits are us shapeshifting into protective armor. This conceals our identity from others.

The tools a plane uses in flight must be adjusted when it's grounded. If the tools are used inversely, hazards arise. Similarly, the "never agains" meant to benefit us risk turning protection into self-sabotage. Good people capable of holding your heart can't reach you, and those who try often grow weary in the process. Our loyalty to these vows causes us to struggle creating and maintaining healthy relationships. Therefore, let's name a few, then determine which ones are ready to be released.

Internal Vows—'Til Healing Do We Part

I've included a mini chart of common vows we hold within because of the challenges we've faced. Read through the vows and see if any apply to you. If not, consider what vows you've made to yourself or others. Then ask yourself the following questions:

1. When have I vowed "never again" to what was hurting me?
2. What does this vow hope to achieve or prevent from happening?

3. What if I didn't need to say "never again" because I've learned how to choose wisely?

The Vow	What It Wants	What It Costs
I won't let anyone see me cry.	Protection from perceived weakness	Disconnection and suppression
I won't ask for help.	Helps you to feel needed or not feel like a burden	Buries your needs and creates resentment
I won't let myself fall apart.	Gives you purpose in chaos	Leaves you emotionally exhausted and unseen
I won't let people get too close.	Prepares you for abandonment	Pushes good people away

When Emotional Vows Become Joint Fulfillments

Michelle and Terrence had their first child at twenty-five. At age forty, the couple had three kids, a mortgage, aging parents to care for, and had forgotten what peace felt like. Their vow? *The kids always come first.* It sounded noble and other parents said it too. They worked hard to give their children a life with fewer gaps, more options, and unconditional love. Michelle often said, "I want to give them what I never had." Terrence agreed. It wasn't just parenting. It was redemption.

The vow slowly morphed from something they chose to something that controlled them. Date nights were constantly postponed. Gym memberships went unused. Michelle stopped painting, and Terrence gave up his Saturday morning jogs. They didn't complain, but their relationship suffered.

Every day was the same: get ready for the day, drop off the kids, go to work, clock out, take the kids to practice, do homework, do house chores, go to bed. The couple said they had an okay marriage, they could resolve arguments, but they weren't truly connected. Conversations revolved around school schedules, pick-ups, drop-offs, and care for their parents. One night, while lying next to each other, Michelle said to Terrence, "Remember when we were younger, and we used to go on dates?" Terrence nodded, and they both went quiet.

What they didn't realize was that their children felt it too. Not through lectures, but through energy, body language, and tone. The air in the home was heavy. The kids noticed how their parents were stressed out, busy, and exhausted. Their son was becoming more distant, and their daughter needed more reassurance than usual. That's because children don't always name stress—they notice it and sometimes internalize it. When parents live on empty, kids start asking: Is love supposed to look like this? Is exhaustion what makes you good? Is it my fault?

Michelle and Terrence's original vow backfired. By not prioritizing each other, their marriage became strained, their personal wellness suffered, and they found themselves burned out. And it negatively impacted their kids. The well-intentioned couple needed a new vow, one that allowed them to regain themselves as individuals, a spouse, and family.

Renewing Vows

Michelle and Terrence decided to have an identity reset. Losing themselves for the sake of their children meant the kids weren't receiving their best mom and dad. Their new vow? "I can prioritize my family alongside myself." At first, the couple thought it was a good idea but not realistic. How could they prioritize themselves without letting someone else down?

They started small. Michelle signed up for an evening art class once a month. Terrence laced up his old sneakers and jogged on Thursday evenings. Together, they created Friday night "porch talks." They talked about their marriage for at least twenty minutes each session. Some weeks, when life really got in the way, they skipped it. But the weeks they didn't? Their marriage felt the difference.

Releasing the emotional vow wasn't dramatic. Admittedly, they struggled to find consistency at first, and the pull to fulfill the old vow won sometimes. Michelle sat in her car outside the art studio, debating whether to go in. Terrence almost canceled his first run. But they went. Not because they were sure it would work out, but because they were curious about how their family would evolve—and who they'd individually become in the process. Their children noticed—not in words, but in the way Michelle laughed more, and how Terrence showed up to their games without looking half asleep.

Renewing Vows Renews You

Michelle and Terrence carried a **Redemptive Parent Identity** built on reform and fear. They were trying to give their children what they never had, but beneath that effort was a subconscious belief: *If we don't love through sacrifice, we'll become the very parents we promised ourselves we'd never be.*

In healing that belief, they grew into a **Present and Whole Identity** that modeled *presence* over performance for their children. This identity is defined by mutual nourishment, where love includes evolution, parenting doesn't require self-abandonment, and presence brings rejuvenation not depletion. This new identity doesn't make them perfect, and their children will likely still say their mom and dad missed the mark sometimes. But it allows their relationship to be a witness of what is possible when we move beyond survival.

However, life is challenging and different for each of us. Not all parents can step into this kind of balance right now. Still, all deserve space to grieve what they've had to carry alone and to imagine a different kind of love that includes themselves. As your capacity expands, most vows don't dissolve—they loosen. You learn that tending to yourself is not dismissing others. It offers them a better version of who you are. *Self-neglect doesn't model love; it models absence.* If you're an over-giver, or one who struggles with self-care, stop making "Who needs me now?" your only go-to question. Instead, ask, "How can I show up in a way that includes me, too?"

Michelle and Terrence's children became better people when their caretakers took care of themselves. When children see parents choose life—not just duty—they learn to do the same. Now this is your invitation to walk differently, to choose vows rooted in identity, not obligation, shame, or fear. The bonus? When your identity shines, everyone around you gets to feel seen.

Trauma Bargaining

Some vows are conscious and intentional. Others are shaped as a reaction to fear, loss, or the moments we couldn't control. When we feel powerless, we bargain. Not with others but with ourselves. I've come to name this pattern a **trauma bargain:** It's a deal you make with yourself after something painful occurs; you trade part of your freedom, expression, or need to feel prepared, safe, or in control. Trauma bargaining doesn't always sound desperate. Sometimes, it sounds responsible. Logical. Even noble. Underneath it is the belief: "I must suffer to protect what's left." It often starts with an emotional vow ("never again will I..."), and the trauma bargain is the life you build around that vow to make sure it holds.

> **The Emotional Vow says:**
> *I got burned, so I'll never touch a hot stove again.*

> **The Trauma Bargain says:**
> *I'm going to stay out of the kitchen all together.*

What does this have to do with identity? Your emotional vows and trauma bargains are visible, even if people cannot articulate them, and they become the identity you're known as. You make an emotional vow that says, "I won't let anyone see me cry," and pair it with the trauma bargain of, "If I stay emotionless, or be happy all the time, they can't use my feelings against me." So, you wear the mask, and before you know it, you're referred to as the "happy one," "not a warm person," "nothing gets to you."

It's no surprise why we hear saddened hearts say, "Everyone thinks nothing bothers me, but I have feelings too!" Others see the vow and clap for you, unaware that a painful bargain you've made has become your life. That's what makes trauma bargains so tricky: They're born from pain, but they look like personality. They can shape how people respond to you—and how you show up in return.

Most of the time, we form them without realizing it. Big life transitions like retirement, having a baby, becoming an empty-nester, and losing someone you love create the perfect storm. The moment is overwhelming. So, you grab the nearest vow for stability. You then build an entire shapeshifting identity around it before considering: Is this really me?

Exploring Commonly Paired Vows and Bargains

The easiest way to recognize our unsupportive actions is by seeing them mirrored in others. We'll do this by viewing the lives of three people.

- Gabriela, who avoids asking for help because she believes her needs are too great.
- Yosef, who assumes closeness always ends in goodbye.
- Franklin, who's convinced rest isn't a state he should submit to.

Notice how their lives aren't extreme or dramatic. They are good, well-intentioned people. That's what makes these situations important. Most trauma bargains don't show up in emergencies. They show up in patterns that become a person's identity.

"I'm a Burden and Afraid to Ask for Help" Pair

Gabriela said it was easy to remember why she stopped asking for help. "My family didn't have much when I was growing up. But I was still a kid. I still had needs. I'd ask for something, and they'd hit me with, 'Don't you know there are kids who starve every night?'"

She looked down, then added, "It made me feel selfish for even asking."

Over time, Gabriela internalized that her needs came at a cost—that every request required justification, and every yes might come with a debt.

"I still feel bad asking for anything," she said crying. "Not just with money, with time, with favors, with care. I don't want to be a burden. And honestly, most times, people can't help anyway. Or they do, and then I feel like I owe them. I don't want that. There's no point in asking for help."

The Emotional Vow: Gabriela's emotional vow formed early. Raised in a household where her parents were often overwhelmed and pressed for resources, she got the message loud and clear: *Don't add to the burden.* The vow she made in the moment of being disappointed and feeling dismissed? "I'll never ask for help again."

When I asked her if anyone in her adulthood extended a helping hand toward her, she told me no. She mentioned how she was exhausted and overwhelmed all the time. She stayed up late trying to finish tasks, woke up extra early to complete them, and rarely had time to herself. I asked her a few more questions, sensing that there was a trauma bargain to follow.

When a new project came up at work, she said, "I've got it," before anyone else could volunteer. She felt anxious sending emails or texts that asked for favors, often deleting them before hitting send. If her significant other asked how she was, she'd say, "I'm good" to avoid having him offer her care. The vow hardened into an emotional bargain.

"I don't owe anybody anything," she said. "What's that saying? If you want a job to get done, do it yourself."

The Trauma Bargain: To keep that vow safe, she struck a quiet deal: "If I never ask, I can't be rejected. If I don't need anyone, no one can use my needs against me."

Gabriela's life reflected the emotional vow and trauma bargain pair. She was always the helper and rarely "the helped." Despite not asking for assistance, she deeply craved it. In some ways, a small part of her imagined, if she did have help, like others did, her life would become more manageable.

Maybe she could relax and have healthier relationships. However, for Gabriela, her pairing had morphed into a pseudo identity that she and others celebrated. Breaking it wasn't easy.

> **The Shapeshifter Mask:** They called her strong, a giving person who was nice.

No one saw the toll. "Does that ever make you angry?" I asked.

She nodded. "I get frustrated because it's not getting any easier. I hate to say it, but I'm resentful. I feel injustice because why do I have to do everything?"

The irony was not lost on her: By refusing help, she'd inadvertently created the very distance she feared. The people she cared about couldn't help because they never knew she needed it. In the silence, the weight of it all continued to press down.

The good news is change begins the moment we're willing to name the thing we've been hiding from. For Gabriela, it was time to peel back the layers of that mask and let herself be seen—not as the strong one, but as the *human* one. The one who needed care as much as she had always given it.

"Everyone Will Eventually Leave" Pair

Yosef said he wanted something lasting: marriage, commitment, legacy. At heart, he said he pictured himself being "a family man," but it seemed that wasn't his fate.

"Every woman I've ever been with has left," he told me. "It was never because of me. It was always them. Their fear. Their drama."

As I listened, I noticed the missing pieces. One woman, the last girlfriend, he said, had texted him every day for a week after a fight.

"I just needed space," he shrugged. "If she couldn't handle that, that's on her."

When I asked him what the pattern had been in past relationships, he didn't hesitate.

"From the first woman to the last," he said, "they all left."

"Who was the first?"

"I don't want to talk about that crap," he said with anger. "This has nothing to do with my mom." Yosef turned his head and started talking about a comedy he had recently watched and asked if I had seen it.

I told him I hadn't, but I was familiar with it. He stopped talking, then checked his watch. I let the silence stretch, knowing something unspoken had brushed the surface. There was a wound beneath the defense. He had come to me to talk about a recent breakup, but his mother showed up in the conversation.

"My father was a good dude. He raised me. He was smart, successful, had a good blue-collar job, but my mom?" He shook his head. "One day she'd pop up and I would see her. I was always happy to be with her. The next few days? Gone."

"It sounds like you were unprepared," I said to him with sadness.

"Of course! Just when I thought she was gonna be around for a bit, something would happen, and she'd leave. But my ex-girlfriend. Whew, boy. I wish you could've met her. She was crazy. One time she. . ." he trailed off again into details.

Yosef's stories revealed a pattern. His relationship had a push-pull dynamic. The two of them would get close to one another, and then something would happen—which he always warranted as "needing a few days off from her."

The Emotional Vow: Sometimes, the grief we bring into new relationships doesn't show up as tears. It shows up as space, anger, or sabotage. Not because we don't want closeness, but because a part of us made a vow: *Never again will I be caught off guard by someone I love leaving.*

Yosef told me he'd spend a day or two of no contact and once, several weeks. Over time, as we continued talking about his relationship struggles, and the grief of not being married yet, thoughts of his mom surfaced.

"I'd be enraged when my mom disappeared. I asked my dad where she went and never received an answer."

"What did you do with all that anger?" I asked him.

"I bottled it up inside, I guess. Played sports. I remember being mad for days though, weeks, however long it took."

It was with those words that he pointed out his trauma bargain and it walked parallel to how he treated his girlfriend. Something would happen, he'd get angry, and instead of her disappearing—he did.

The Trauma Bargain: To keep his vow safe, he struck a deal: "If I leave first, then no one can reject or abandon me. I won't feel helpless, and I can get ahead of the hurt by becoming the one who goes missing."

At some point, the absence becomes familiar. Not only theirs but yours, too. You don't mean to leave emotionally, mentally, or physically. A part of you believes it's safer that way. You think you're creating space, giving things time to cool. What you're doing, though, is building a buffer between now and disappointment.

Yosef didn't realize it, but his silence was his way of trying to stay in control and protect his dignity. Grief that's never grieved doesn't vanish, it replays. Sometimes, we don't see that we've become the very thing we feared: the one who disappears without warning.

> **The Shapeshifter Mask:** They said he keeps to himself. That he shows up when he wants to and engages on his terms. They called him easygoing. He called it being logical—measured.

Unfortunately, ghosting has become culturally accepted. Many promote it as an act of empowerment, reframing it as "healing." But is it? In cases of abuse, chronic harm, or real threat, disappearing is a form of self-protection. Silence is survival when safety is compromised. However, most ghosting isn't about danger. It's about dysregulation.

It's the nervous system doing what it knows best: shut down, disappear, and avoid the discomfort of rupture. The body goes into fight or flight mode, and fleeing feels the safest. Healing allows us to understand that what was safe when we were younger may be detrimental to our character and relationships in the present.

Through sessions, Yosef realized it wasn't that his ex-girlfriend "couldn't handle it," as he initially thought.

Instead, what he called a boundary was really a survival strategy—a way to manage emotional overwhelm without the tools to cope with it directly. His nervous system didn't know how to navigate conflict. It didn't know how to face the discomfort of a messy, vulnerable conversation without pulling away.

Sometimes, people don't have the language or the courage to name this. They don't know how to end something without disappearing from it. The good news is this isn't permanent. I've seen my clients grow beyond this. Over time, they learn that ruptures can be mended and that true emotional maturity lies in the repair work.

For Yosef, the realization didn't come all at once. It wasn't a single moment of clarity. It happened slowly. Each time he ghosted someone, a little more of the truth became clear. Eventually, in one of our sessions, he said, "I never wanted to be the one who disappears." In that small, simple statement, I could see the shift. It wasn't only about understanding the pattern anymore. It was about feeling how deeply it had shaped him and how he longed to finally show up, even when the fear of abandonment loomed.

"I Can't Afford to Slow Down or Rest" Pair

Franklin didn't consider himself a workaholic. He was just "driven." He liked crossing things off lists and being the one people could count on. In his private moments—when the dishes were done, the inbox was cleared, and there was nowhere else to be—something strange would happen. His chest would tighten like a jammed drawer that refused to open. His mind would scan for something else to do. His body, wired from habit, wouldn't let him exhale.

"I don't know how to just. . . rest," he said once. "Even when I've earned it. Even when I'm so tired I could cry."

He wasn't new to burnout, but the grind had intensified after his divorce. The settlement had been fair, technically. He got to keep his dignity but lost the financial cushion that helped him breathe. He didn't talk much about what he gave up. It wasn't the house or the shared savings, but the sense of future ease he thought he'd earned.

Now, though he made good money, his nervous system stayed in a near-constant state of alert. Rest became a threat and stillness felt reckless. Instead, Franklin picked up extra consulting hours—"just in case," and people praised him for his ambition. They called him sharp, dependable, and consistent. Franklin wasn't chasing success anymore, though. He was running from the feeling of collapse.

The Emotional Vow: After his divorce, a vow was made deep inside Franklin's body: "*Never again will I allow myself to go without.*" It was less about wealth and more about control. He had spent so much time thinking he was stable. He had done everything "right," and still, it all shifted.

Franklin didn't want to feel that kind of vulnerability again. If he worked enough, prepared enough, *earned enough*—he believed he could keep the bottom from falling out. If he wasn't responding to messages or tightening up a spreadsheet, he was tackling home projects, helping a neighbor move, or taking on a new hobby before finishing the last. "I like staying productive," he'd say. Even his hobbies came with goals, and his downtime had a to-do list. He couldn't just watch a movie—he needed to clean while it played. Rest had to be paired with progress.

When he stopped to rest something uneasy stirred inside. Guilt. Dread. The sense that he should be doing something better, more useful, or more important. Stillness made him restless. Productivity made him feel safe. Though the world praised him for being dependable and driven, Franklin feared what might rise to the surface if he ever truly let himself slow down. What looked like motivation was a nervous system trying to outrun itself.

> **The Trauma Bargain:** To keep his vow safe, he struck a quiet deal: "If I stay in motion, I won't have to face the discomfort underneath the stillness." It was Franklin's way of protecting himself from anxiety, grief, and guilt.

Rest wasn't restful—it was noisy, and the list of what he felt he should be doing kept popping up in the background. When he finally tried to relax, it felt undeserved. Although his body was exhausted, and his mind was foggy, relaxing was impossible. Like many, Franklin fantasized about rest and then sabotaged it when the opportunity arrived. Rest, for Franklin, was both the medicine and the trigger.

Franklin's story isn't unusual. In a world that idolizes hustle, fear is often mislabeled as ambition. We praise those who "push through," "never stop," and "make it look easy." But when our worth becomes tied to what we produce, exhaustion follows. True success isn't the work we create—it's the wholeness of the person behind it. And like Franklin, many find themselves weary at a soul level.

The Shapeshifter Mask: People called him high achieving. He smiled when they said it. His mask was being the capable one who could do more with less.

The trouble is, when the thing that soothes you is also the thing that stings, you get stuck in a loop. Franklin's nervous system needed permission to learn safety differently—through releasing the doing and embracing the ability to "just be."

Reviewing Your Contracts

As depicted in the stories of Gabriela, Yosef, and Franklin, we each have made emotional vows and trauma bargains. In business or in our personal lives, we take time to review contracts and terms and conditions when circumstances change. Take a moment to review the contracts you've made. Like any deal, we can't get a better one if we're unaware of the one we're bound to. The following graphic allows you to see what we quietly and subconsciously sign up for.

Here's What Lies Behind the Shapeshifter's Mask

The Vow	A Kinder Reframe	What It Gives You
"If I carry everyone, maybe I won't be left."	"I'm allowed to belong without constantly proving my value."	Spaciousness, reciprocity, emotional relief

The Vow	A Kinder Reframe	What It Gives You
"I always have to be the strong one."	"I can be strong *and* supported."	Shared responsibility, deeper self-worth
"If I expect nothing, I can't be let down."	"I can hold hope *with* caution."	Healthy expectations, earned joy
"Everyone leaves eventually."	"Some people leave—but some stay."	Openness to secure attachment
"I'm better off alone."	"Alone may feel safer, but I want to learn what it's like to feel safe *with*."	Growth through community, co-regulation
"I can't afford to fall apart."	"I'm allowed to soften. I don't have to perform okay-ness."	Rest, regulation, healing without collapse

Once you've been made aware of the terms, ask yourself: How do I feel about this deal? Is this something I want to review for the next year, five years, or more? If not, there's a way to change this.

Your Agreement

1. **Emotional Vow**
   I once made this vow:
   Never again will I ______________________.

2. **Trauma Bargain**
   To uphold that vow, I struck this bargain:
   If I ______________________,
   then I won't have to ______________________.

3. Shapeshifter Mask
To protect this agreement, I often became: ____________________.

4. Benefit of Revising
By revising this contract, I gain: ____________.

Undoing the Deal

The purpose of self-awareness is freedom, not shame. You weren't meant to fashion yourself according to pain but around truth. That's why undoing the deals we've contracted is necessary. Self-awareness is only a gift if you steward it with supportive actions. To be perpetually conscious of pain without methods to heal or relieve it is agonizing.

For me, I came to know myself like the winter knows trees—by what was stripped away. I looked at my life and saw the shape I had taken out of need rather than choice or joy. I exchanged one negative consequence for another. Through everyday conversations with people, I've learned this is not a personal flaw but a human adaptation. We assess alternative ways to get love, find peace, fill our stomachs, and end quarrels. We seek out relationships that help us avoid being in isolation and strategies that promise to prevent another heartbreak. In the end, we all share the same innate desire: to feel safe while being our true selves. Compromise occurs when that isn't possible.

Life is harsh but ironically, turning toward what others want is easy. We become moldable to what we're directly or indirectly told to do. Society teaches you how to grieve, how to succeed, and how to tuck your pain in like a clean shirt at sunrise. Somewhere inside of you, your roots pull in discomfort. When you have forgotten, your soul remembers that you had your own way once. That remembering is the beginning of reconstruction. It's the quiet awareness that signals something deeper in you is ready to rebuild. For now, it's enough to notice where your vows and bargains began. Later, in the Builder Root, you'll be invited to reimagine what they could become. You'll turn these restrictions into practices that restore your wholeness.

Friendly Recap

- **Awareness and revision of emotional contracts:** You've made emotional vows and survival agreements that have shaped how you show up in the world. By identifying these patterns, you can decide whether to keep them or rewrite them to align more authentically with who you truly are.
- **The power of undoing old patterns:** The masks we wear often come from a place of survival and protection, but these outdated strategies may now limit us. Letting go of the need to please others or fit in creates space for self-acceptance and healthier relationships.
- **Growth through self-awareness and action:** True freedom comes when you not only recognize the emotional deals you've made but actively revise them. Self-awareness alone is not enough—it's the courageous choice to rewrite your internal agreements and embrace your true self that brings lasting change.

Root Two

THE TRUTH SEEKER

Come Sit with Me

After a loss, the last thing you need is for the know-it-alls to arrive. You know who I'm referring to. The "I told you so" committee and the "you should have known" tribe. People who serve the truth cold and without emotional seasoning.

Sure, people say they're "keeping it real" and that "the truth hurts," but I disagree. The truth doesn't cause pain; shame does. When you're sitting around the dinner table and someone points out all the truths they see about you, it's not the honesty you remember. It's the hurt feelings and embarrassment. You see their disapproving faces paired with uncomfortable silence. It tells a story, and one that says, "This doesn't feel good. All of me might not be welcomed here." That's because when honesty comes from a true, *loving* place, it's like honey, easier to digest and disarming.

People like you don't need *tough* love. People like you deserve *kind* love. A cradle to the heart, a massage to the mind, a pillow for the bones. When truth is delivered with harshness, it brings anxiety and unrelenting guilt. It leads you to fear honest words. You hide from what others see in you and the unpleasantness you see in yourself. That's why when you're hurting, you reach for comfort. For softness. Or at least for someone to say, "This sucks, and I'm here to help you along the way."

Your heart doesn't want more criticism than you've already been given. And nearly no one has beaten you up worse than you have. The soul longs for someone who understands you with such profoundness, they acknowledge you've done the best you could with what you had. They honor how your intentions were rooted in love, even when your internal capacity was too limited to express it. Now, this isn't an excuse for how your actions impacted people, but it is a permission slip to forgive yourself. Lasting growth isn't about denying harm—it's about being honest enough to repair it. And that kind of honesty requires softness.

Yet, you and I know that the truth doesn't always sink into us like warm tea on a cold day. Instead, it's inconvenient. It shows up mid-chaos, mid-healing, mid-heartbreak, and unfiltered. It doesn't matter if the day's been long, or if you've finally mustered enough will to try again. Truth shows up like a child—uncaring and without social cues. You're at a party and your son yells out, "Mom, you left your laxatives on the toilet."

Dang, why are you shouting out my business? Now everyone knows I'm backed up and brokenhearted. That's what truth feels like when it lacks tenderness. It's not just the content that hurts—it's the lack of tone, timing, and delivery. The discomfort is distressing. We don't want to face it, and we sure enough don't want others to discover it.

The Truth Seeker Root

When the fog of life begins to lift—when your mind feels a little less cluttered and illusions recede—the Truth Seeker Root extends downward and laterally. We look back with regret. But hindsight is not a weapon; it's a window. It's a view of the roads you've walked barefoot, bleeding and wounded, brave but unsure, resilient yet exhausted. And when you look ahead, the path might not look brighter yet. This is where frustration and the temptation to give up arrive; we confuse the tension of our expansion as evidence of us breaking. This isn't a setback; it's you being grounded. I've coined it "the oh-hell-nah" phase. Welcome to the Messy Middle of Transition, friend, where clarity smacks you on one side and embraces you on the other.

You start having aha moments when you least expect it. At work. At Target. Mid-therapy and while folding the laundry you meant to do yesterday. The Truth Seeker Root becomes your internal compass. It holds your intuition and discernment—the ability to recognize the almost right thing from the real thing. It doesn't shout. It doesn't rush. It's your inner knowing. However, when truth first activates, it feels like a threat. Its invitation says, *Come closer. Look again. See what lies beneath.* The thought of that can feel scary. What if I don't like what appears? What if I don't know how to fix myself or change? What if I can't? What if it's too overwhelming and causes me to spiral into places I barely escaped last time? What if I never recover?

When the Truth Feels Scary

These are all natural questions and important ones to ask. The Truth Seeker Root knows this. So, it gently guides you through trauma-informed truth-telling. It's the art of hearing and speaking truth without shutting down, running away, collapsing, or freezing up. It respects the uncalloused edges of your capacity—the invisible boundary between what you can hold and what makes you feel overburdened. Psychology calls this your "window of tolerance."[1] But in everyday speak, liken it to how much accountability and disillusion you can bench-press *without* suffering. To keep you safe during this process, healthy truth-sharing applies the following logic:

- Vulnerability is a gift, not a weapon.
- Honesty should be encouraged, not punished.

---

[1] Siegal, D. (1999). *The Developing Mind: How Relationships and the Brain Interact to Shape Who We Are*. New York: Guilford Press.

- Create safety when the truth is hard to hear. Without it, people tend to shut down or get defensive.
- The goal isn't to expose you—it's to help you *see* what's working, and what's not. True self-awareness highlights your weaknesses *and* your strengths.

Truth is powerful, but because it can heal or harm, trauma-informed truth-telling is important. If at any point you need to rest, put these words down, and return to them. Sometimes we need to digest in small portions or have an appetizer before diving into the full meal. Also know that there isn't any way to make every word, and every sentence, apply to you. As I tell my clients, "If it doesn't apply, let it fly." You might store it in your back pocket as "something I might use." Or you can decide something said isn't right for you. Again, the best part about the Truth Seeking Root is that it gives *you* power—power to say "no, this isn't for me," and "I want to read into this more."

The Truth Seeker Root helps you spot patterns you used to walk right into. You pause before saying yes out of guilt. You stop calling exhaustion "strength" just to keep going. You feel less shaken when someone disagrees with you or pulls away. You no longer need to rehearse conversations to justify your truth. Instead, clarity looks like:

- Detecting manipulation and guilt-tripping faster
- Trusting your "no" without guilt and your "yes" without hesitation
- Making confident decisions without others' constant input
- Defining yourself by the good things that happened to you, rather than the bad
- Grieving, healing, or growing on your own without needing permission from others

More than anything, truth-seeking brings relief. Not because it erases grief, but because it gives you something loss and trauma often steals: the ability to trust again. This root brings clarity, not from having all the answers, but from no longer needing to wrestle with confusion. Misunderstandings you've long held begin to clear.

However, this root doesn't grow in comfort. It grows in the wilderness. The Truth Seeker thrives in quiet places where distractions aren't abundant and illusions break down. Where you're no longer numbed by noise, and all that's left is *you* and what's *true*. Please know you don't have to master this root all at once. Just remember: the Truth Seeker Root is here to help you see clearly and without shaming yourself. Now, let us begin.

Chapter 4

The Weight of What's True Now

You can't shout at a tomato seed to make it grow faster. You can't force the sunrise to awaken the earth quicker than it will. Some things, especially those that are valuable, often need presence to unfold. Grief is one of them. Healing is another. When it comes to handling the truth, we must slow down to notice it.

Honesty speaks in the body—through the lump in your throat, the tension behind your eyes, the nervous energy that makes you scroll, pace, or shut down. Truth is always speaking, but it tends to whisper. The Truth Seeker Root distributes truth in small portions because bearing the weight of it all at once would be overwhelming. Yet, what if the portions are also cumbersome? How do you sit with what's hard?

- The reality that the relationship is over.
- The thought of, "I should be further along."

- The frustration of I'm not who I was, and I'm also not who I want to be.

These aren't annoyances and sad feelings. They're grief. Therapeutic spaces say "feel your feelings," but what comes after that? Being in a state of mental fog isn't fun, and the way out requires adjustment. The scary part is you've already undergone a lifetime of upheaval. Inviting more alterations, good ones included, feels like asking for the other shoe to drop. Who wants that? As much as the phrases "Change is good!" or "Change is necessary!" is thrown around, we often lack the tools needed to grow our capacity and endure the distress change brings.

It's no wonder then why we don't celebrate becoming more of ourselves. Evolving isn't a trip to the spa. Do you know how much I wish someone said to me, "Ooooh girl, just rub a little eucalyptus oil on your trauma, you'll be fine!" Instead, our true self walks in, takes inventory, and demands that we retire the version of ourself that got us through hell. The fear is *What if I need that version?* Life doesn't stop throwing arrows.

Listen, I get it, friend, but healing doesn't mean letting go of strength. *Healing means letting go of unnecessary suffering. It gives you the chance to feel the pain without becoming the wound.* We either learn how to take hold of what hurts or let what hurts take hold of us.

Why Accepting the Truth Is Hard

Truths fall into two categories: those we are happy to hear, and others that are uncomfortable to receive. What we don't admit is how these truths impact how we see ourselves and cause internal conflict. You discover a file you didn't know existed, a message pops up at 2:00 a.m., information from a conversation you weren't supposed to hear reveals life-changing details. We name these as betrayal, the guilt of what we missed, the regret of what can't be returned, and the frustration of *why did I ignore that?* It's when reality collides with what we've hoped for.

When your body doesn't feel safe, rarely will it let you leap into something new without a fight—no matter how badly your mind wants to. That's why I tell practitioners: There is no such thing as a resistant person, only an armored one who doesn't feel safe. Unprocessed experiences create invisible guardrails that makes forward motion difficult. The well-respected psychologist Dr. Peter Levine writes in his book *Waking the Tiger: Healing Trauma,* "Traumatic symptoms are not caused by the 'triggering' event itself. They stem from the frozen residue of energy that has not been resolved and discharged; this residue remains trapped in the nervous system."[1]

This is why grief follows truths, and acceptance grows alongside healing. Grief isn't the enemy; it's the process your body moves through to make sense of what happened, and who you are now because of it. Expressing what hurts is the release; when we suppress pain, it slowly harms us emotionally, physiologically, and spiritually. Being honest about what hurts allows us to understand the pain. Sadly, today's culture limits whose sorrow is allowed. We teach boys not to cry and that "being a man" means cutting off emotional intelligence at the root. We've taught girls not to get angry, praised the "strong Black woman" while ignoring her exhaustion, and dismissed Indigenous people diagnosed with depression without considering the history of their pain. We call neurodivergent people "too sensitive" and expect them to adjust instead

---

[1] Levine, P.A. (1997). *Waking the Tiger: Healing Trauma: The Innate Capacity to Transform Overwhelming Experiences.* North Atlantic Books.

of asking the world to expand. The list of emotional restraint only grows when we consider nuances such as age, income, family culture, and biology—all of which culture uses to determine who gets to emote what and when.

No wonder we power through agony, overthink it, or numb it with distraction, only to feel lost when those habits stop holding us together. The distress happens when we internally ask, "What happened? I've always been able to get through. What's going on now?" *Grief slows us down not to punish us, but to guide us.* Maybe that's the point.

> *Resetting your identity isn't about getting back to who you were but learning how to stay present with who you are, especially in the spaces where you feel most undone.*

This is the work of becoming: We don't rush the sunrise. We don't yell at the seed. We stay long enough to witness what grows.

To Give and Receive Truth, We Must First Be Present

Presence is a prerequisite for truth-telling—for both the giver and the receiver. To embrace the truth, you don't need better arguments; you need more safety, more courage, and more presence. Our willingness to explore what lies beneath our defenses and self-doubt determines how much clarity we gain from our relationships. With the world ever-changing and fear rising, many of us find ourselves *being there* rather than *being present*. Yet receiving truth isn't an act of forcing; it's an act of welcome.

When you're standing in the checkout line at the grocery store, you notice the people around you—you're aware of their existence. But if the person in front of you turns around, catches your tired eyes, and says, "Oh, you only have a few items. Go in front of me," that's presence. Presence notices not just what's happening, but *who* it's happening to. When someone is present, not only do they witness your circumstances. They witness *you*. More than anything, presence begins with how you lovingly embrace yourself.

However, sometimes the truth is hard to hear either because you've never felt comfortable enough to share it or safe enough to receive it. So how do you start? You begin gently. For some, noticing the truth in others will feel safer. Seeing someone turn on the light of truth within themselves gives us permission to do the same. For others, seeing the truth resting inside us feels easier to hold. You might have to experiment with each to see where your strong suit is. And yes, I recommend starting with your strengths to boost courage and confidence. Then, you can slowly touch the areas that feel more vulnerable and uneasy. (Remember: This isn't about fixing what's wrong with you—it's about discovering what's right with you and strengthening other aspects of yourself to decrease the power fear and shame have held over you.)

Presence Encourages You to Consider

When the moment arises for you to tell someone the truth, whether it's you offering feedback they've requested or something you want to bring to their attention, appraise the situation. In a house appraisal, the appraiser considers all the various elements of a house: Where is it located? What condition is it *already* in? What work *needs* to be done? What's *unique* about the home? What's the *benefit* of living here?

Before offering a truth to someone, consider the "condition" of their emotional state and what they've been through: Are they grieving? In rage where they likely won't hear? Driving? Where are they located? Alone, with friends, or sitting in my office as I deliver a diagnosis? What's the benefit of telling them? Is it to feed my ego or to support them? What's unique about this person? Where can I offer positive affirmation or support?

If someone offers you feedback, you can respond—out loud or internally—"Thanks for sharing that. I'll consider it." The word *consider* in Greek is *katamanthano* (kat-am-an-than'-o), which means "to learn thoroughly, to examine carefully and accurately." That's presence in action. When truth surfaces, ask: Is this accurate? Where is it coming from? What does it stir in me—and why? Not every truth requires action. Some truths are seeds, not instructions.

I went to a teacher's conference on behalf of the health organization I was working for at the time. I got into small-talk with one middle school teacher and asked him, "What is most rewarding about your profession?" He told me about a student in his seventh-grade math class. The child was a solid B-student who rarely caused trouble. Toward the end of the school year, he noticed the student's grades were dropping.

"Those Bs turned into Cs and Ds," he said. "At first, I figured he was getting like most almost-graduates, slacking off, but I decided to ask him what was happening." The teacher told me that the student was struggling not because of laziness, but circumstance.

"My student told me they lived in a violent home, and to make matters worse, the light bill had gone unpaid. He said he'd sit on the bathroom floor to do his homework because it was the only place he could find peace and quiet. With the electricity off, and no window in the bathroom, he couldn't see. It wasn't that the kid wasn't applying himself. He didn't have a good, stable environment to complete his schoolwork."

The teacher went on to say he volunteered to stay at the school late so his student could complete his math assignments and coursework for other classes. Having someone take the time to see his situation and show up made the difference between graduating and being left behind.

As you see, presence doesn't always mean stillness. Presence can be active. For the student, it looked like someone taking time to understand him. For the teacher, the Truth Seeker Root looked like challenging his preconceived assumption: "The kid is simply slacking off." If we apply this same ability to ourselves, we can consider how who we are today has been shaped by the opportunities, environments, life situations, and victories we've experienced. Maybe life looks messy because somewhere, the lights got turned off in your life, and you were left to find another way to thrive.

To Give and Receive Truth, We Must Stay Curious

The next time you're tempted to judge someone, get curious. You'll notice that it's hard to simultaneously pass judgment while asking a genuine question. In fact, the opposite of assumption is curiosity. You've likely heard of "the nosey neighbor" or someone who's always "all up in somebody's business." Let's bring clarity:

- Curiosity isn't a posture of suspicion.
- Curiosity isn't for gossip, drama, control, or personal gain.
- Real curiosity brings connection.
- Real curiosity leaves the door open without demanding anyone to walk through it.

How is curiosity linked with grief, loss, and personal identity? *While shame uses the truth to deliver a verdict, curiosity uses truth to usher in understanding.* Thoughts that someone's been "grieving too long" or that they "need to get over it" gets dismantled when you understand the pain they're in. Judging yourself by asking, "What's wrong with me?" withers when you instead ask, "What happened that shaped this belief?" Curiosity remembers there's a person behind the pain. It sees their story.

Mark was a young teen I met in a mentorship program. He struggled with fitting in and making friends.

"People judge me because they don't know my story," he told me.

Mark was a good kid and the best among them. He'd say "thank you" at times people normally wouldn't express gratitude. He'd ask questions to seek a deeper meaning of something seemingly insignificant; he was happy to help those who were in need. Yet, I saw the overwhelm he carried out as he finished the school year. Midway through, his mother had died.

"My birth mom gave me up when I was a kid. Someone found me on the street. I hadn't eaten and I guess it impacted my health," he said. "I might be a little slow, but I was forced to see the harsher side of life fast." Mark let out a long sigh, then looked back up at me.

"The woman who I called mother had adopted me. Then she died. I told some of my friends in class my life story and they all felt bad. Everyone started apologizing to me for how they treated me, including some teachers."

My heart felt heavy and sad for Mark, and while it might've seemed normal to feel happy that others were finally starting to embrace him, his body told a different story. Every time he mentioned how people were being kind to him, he bawled up his fists and scrunched up his face. What he said stayed with me.

"I shouldn't have to tell people my life's story in order for them to accept me as I am," Mark said.

I wonder how many of us have an "inner Mark"—a part of us that we hide or judge because we don't feel comfortable accepting it. How many of us encounter a Mark whom we dismiss or hold preconceived notions toward? Curiosity invites us to meet both ourselves and others with gentleness. It doesn't demand a confession; it offers connection. When we stay curious, we honor the parts of every story that grief has touched and every truth that's still unfolding. In doing so, we make room for compassion—the soil where healing and identity can take root.

What Is This Emotion Trying to Show Me?

Emotion	What It Might Be Saying	What It Might Need
Anxiety	I'm afraid something bad is coming.	**Reassurance.** Wise preparation (if possible). A reminder that you're not powerless.
Anger/ Protest	Something valuable was taken from me. I feel disrespected or unheard. This isn't fair.	**Protection.** The courage to advocate for yourself and uphold healthy boundaries. Understanding from others.
Grief	I've lost someone, something, or a dream that mattered to me.	**Comfort.** Permission to mourn, and to express your thoughts and emotions safely.
Frustration	I feel stuck or unseen in a situation that isn't changing.	**Validation or movement.** A new path or goals to switch direction.
Despair	I'm tired of hoping and losing.	**Compassion.** Room to rest and gentle restoration of small wins.
Insecurity	I'm afraid I'm not enough or that I'll be exposed.	**Affirmation and confidence.** Knowing your strengths and feeling safe to make mistakes as you learn.
Numbness	It's too much. I shut down to prevent feeling overwhelmed.	**Safe containment.** Slowly learning how to feel in small, manageable portions.

Emotion	What It Might Be Saying	What It Might Need
Jealousy	I see something I long for that makes me ache over what I don't have.	**Acknowledgment of longing.** Permission to have what you yearn for or grieve what was taken.
Disappointment	What I trusted and expected to happen didn't.	**Acceptance and release.** Grieving what didn't happen, then accepting it. Then releasing the "what others/myself should be."
Guilt	I survived, healed, changed, and part of me feels wrong for it. I should have done something different.	**Permission and compassion.** Understanding you did what you knew to do in the past, and you don't have to pay an eternal debt for what happened.

The Truth Seeker Root unravels a story of self-understanding and compassion. Curiosity helps us understand what we need, not what survival taught us to settle for. Emotions make sense when we listen to the message they're telling us. When we see a child cry for their parent, perhaps they aren't always acting out. Maybe it's their way of saying, "I miss you. I need a safe connection." Curiosity helps us hear ourselves the same way.

Another method of getting curious is asking, *When have I felt this way before?* This opens the pathway to self-awareness.

Survival stories aren't bad. They're incomplete.

I once had a client, Nadia, whose best friend died suddenly. One day she was here, the next day she was gone. That's scary. It shows that even when "life is good" it can be taken away without notice or warning. As she started to build new friendships, she sent a text to an acquaintance who didn't respond right away. Her mind spiraled into a million places: *Did she die, too? Maybe she's ignoring me? Perhaps she doesn't want to be friends? What did I do wrong?*

I asked her, "Have you felt this fear before?"

She paused, then nodded. "The day my friend died," she said. "I was texting and calling her, but she never answered. When I finally got through, it was a relative who picked up—to tell me she was gone."

Another memory followed. "I think my mom used to do something similar," she added quietly. "When I was little and she came home from work upset, she'd go silent—wouldn't talk to me at all."

"So, somewhere along the way you learned that silence means danger."

"Yes, that's it. I guess so."

"What if someone's silence doesn't mean 'something is wrong with me,' or 'the person is dead,' but instead, they have a personal challenge they're dealing with or genuinely unavailable?"

Nadia smiled a little. "I never thought about that." She paused for a minute.

Nadia had learned to interpret silence as "I've messed things up," when truthfully, silence often says more about the other person's reality than it does about her worth. Her story wasn't just about abandonment. It was about a little girl who needed protection and learned to stay alert to survive. Curiosity helps you finally hear the parts of you that never stopped longing for safety and love. For Nadia, this meant loosening an old survival belief and glimpsing a new one: I retain my value regardless of who is present.

Before you can change who you are, you have to be honest about the "me you see." If that view is distorted by shame, trauma, or an unmet need, healing won't stick. The Truth Seeker Root allows us to reframe, dismantle shame, and validate what's tender. It allows us to see parts of ourselves in others and the valuable aspects they carry within. Honesty becomes a gift—it allows you to honor the story of what happened to you, without letting it define who you are. Truth reveals the "you" that's always been there, hidden beneath the versions life demanded you become. Once you become aware of that, you gain a profound power: the ability to distinguish what narratives are yours to carry and which ones you can lay down.

The Gift of Presence

Presence makes room for flexibility, including when the path isn't one you've chosen. Death interrupts the best-laid plans. It steals relationships, careers, dreams of children, homes we longed for—and, sometimes, the people we loved most. Life, too, finds ways to interrupt us: a family member needing a ride, a boss asking us to stay late, a patient calling in crisis. In my work with clients and in my own life, I've learned that true presence requires something deeper than stillness or attentiveness. It requires flexibility—the ability to be inconvenienced and show up without an agenda.

Presence waits, listens, adjusts. It invites us to stay a little longer in a conversation we didn't plan for, or to sit with a new insight we've discovered about ourselves. The Truth Seeker Root invites us to move more slowly through someone else's story—and our own.

When you meet life without force—without rushing yourself, your healing, or anyone else's process—you make room for truth to emerge. Presence without an agenda welcomes honesty. It deepens your capacity to face uncertainty, to fail and recover, and to trust yourself again. It says, "I can bend without breaking. I can be disrupted without being destroyed and betraying myself." That's the kind of person your Truth Seeking Root helps you become.

Friendly Recap

Presence doesn't force truth to appear. It simply creates a safe place for it to surface. Shame thrives when we label ourselves as wrong, broken, or bad. Loving curiosity seeks to understand you, not hurt you. Questions to ask:

1. What's one truth you've come to recognize about yourself? Is there a place in your life where you're being invited to slow down and listen?
2. What does the hurting part of you need most right now—comfort, courage, rest, or something else?

Chapter 5

Tolerating the Distress of Change

I never imagined how much grief comes with knowing the truth. The sadness of realizing a friendship would collapse when you stopped overgiving and asked for reciprocity. The frustration of tracing your fear of rejection back to your parents. The grief of burying your spouse and learning about their infidelity. We all want honesty, but few talk about the pain that comes with clarity. After loss, change, and survival, we lose the falsehoods that upheld our identities.

Added to that are the truths that expose us. We reflect on the unkind things we said when we were hurting. The ways we controlled our kids under the guise of protecting them. The times we ignored our gut because someone else's comfort mattered more than ours. Sometimes it feels better to blame others because we don't want to accept our imperfections.

This dismantling of illusions creates pathways for the Truth Seeker Root to flourish. We don't always welcome its growth. We want to avoid it, run away, or distract ourselves until we're numb. When you're already in a painful place in life, or making your way out of one, the last place you want to be is in between what was and what is.

Internal Truths: The Wasteland

After you've grown exhausted of being everything to everyone and wearing masks to keep them happy, you find yourself in the wilderness. A place that strips you of friends, family relationships, and perhaps, your confidence and willpower. Your internal world feels empty. There's an eeriness you can't describe, and your surety has been replaced with confusion and decision fatigue. You look at what you've lost, and all else in comparison teeters between being a small thing or a monumental crisis.

You don't cry as often in the wilderness, and when you do, it feels like the tears have dried up. You wonder if people notice your struggles or that the smile on your face is borrowed and forced. You're not sure what you believe anymore. You're not sure who's safe to talk to. You're not even sure what kind of future you want now. The desert feels endless at first. You wonder if you'll ever see life on the other side of it. But this emptiness is where your truth begins to settle, and it's here where you can finally hear yourself again.

The wasteland doesn't last forever, but you might not see that yet. As you grieve your internal world, your external one is changing, and that can feel unbearable. You start feeling the tiredness that comes with acknowledging *what was really going on* all along. The truth that no one showed up. That you didn't know how to ask for what you needed. That you had to survive in ways you're now paying for. This is the beginning of seeing clearly because deserts don't just take things. Truth reveals what *happened*, it reveals what you *allowed*, what you *ignored*, what you can't control and undo. It regurgitates what you swallowed to keep a peace that never came. It's overwhelming. No one tells you that insight comes with heartbreak.

So, let's establish this early: This isn't failure. You're not lost because you messed up. You're in the desert because you stopped pretending your old life worked. Or you were forced out of it. And that's okay. Not knowing who to be yet is uncomfortable, but not a crime. You're not here to be perfect. You're here to be honest.

Fewer experiences show us how to be raw and unyielding to our heart's integrity than the pain of change.

Early in my journey, when the brain fog started to clear up and I saw life as it truly was, I wasn't happy—I was shaken. It didn't take long to realize denial was easier. No wonder we say, "Ignorance is bliss" and leave off the second half of the phrase, "'tis folly to be wise." The death of anything robs you of innocence and naivety and the belief that most things, if not all, are wonderful. Truth feels like a wasteland that leaves us asking, "What was it all for? What's the point of anything now? Whatever I had to gain came attached to more loss."

Remaining Versus Giving Up

Remember, the brain doesn't care if you're happy, it only wants you to survive. If learning and adjusting to something new requires more momentum and brain energy, while you're already running on low, the path of least resistance looks like going back to what you're used to. That could be the friendships that revealed themselves after a death in the family. The bad habits you picked up along the way to distract yourself or pass time. How your marriage operated when you decided to avoid conflict or be uncompromising.

To combat going back to old habits, name what comfort they gave you, not just what they cost you.

It wasn't the pattern you were attached to; it was the identity it gave you. Being the one who forgave quickly made you feel morally grounded or religiously faithful. Being the one who laughed everything off made you feel like nothing got to you. Being the griever who dreaded the idea of no longer being miserable gave you proof that your pain mattered.

Asking you to acknowledge this truth? It doesn't just feel like change. It feels like loss or maybe a personal attack you're ready to defend yourself against. If I admit that's true, does that mean parts of my pain once felt like home? This is the tipping point: the moment we either retreat or choose something different. Something softer. We can build a home that isn't made of pain but still leaves room for it. *You don't have to live inside of grief; you can let grief live inside of you.*

As we consider change, it's easy to think we should just *force* ourselves into the next chapter. We think that, somehow, by pushing past the discomfort, we'll be better off. Sometimes, we resist the Truth Seeker Root from taking up residence. I was reminded of this when I saw my late grandmother walking as if she was in pain.

My family had gotten Grandma a new mattress, and it was great. I'm talking about orthopedic, chiropractor-approved, presidential-sleep-chambers great. So, when I saw her walking like she had cinder blocks for muscles, I asked her what was wrong.

"Oh, I'm just a little stiff from sleeping in my chair," she said.

IN. HER. CHAIR. Huh? "Grandma, you have a brand-new mattress. It's comfortable. Why are you sleeping in your chair?"

"The bed has a wobbly leg, and I ain't 'bout to roll off of it and wake up to see God or the E.R."

I shook my head and laughed. I said, "All right, we'll fix it." I called my brother, and he came over after work. He shook the bed a little, then started swapping things out like a NASCAR pit stop. He got on the ground and tightened the screws, bolts, legs—everything. Hell, I think he tightened the floor. Grandma's bed wasn't going anywhere.

The next morning, I went to check up on her and guess where she was? Yup. In her chair. "Grandma! Why are you sleeping here again?" I asked her.

She looked up at me like *I* was the problem.

"AJ fixed your bed yesterday, remember?"

"I saw what he did, but I ain't sleepin' on it. You come over at 2:00 a.m. and try it out. Report back and let me know how it goes!" She threw her head back and closed her eyes.

That's Grandma logic for you. It doesn't matter if you show her proof, she needs a full testimonial and a signed affidavit from Jesus to consider it. Why? Pain was predictable. Grandma sat in that chair like a queen on her throne. She wasn't moving and you dared not make her.

Yet, that's how we operate after trauma and loss. *We get comfortable with what's painful because it's familiar. Even when we know better, we might choose to stay with the old pain rather than risk the foreign territory of healing*. Numbing ourselves to stay where we are isn't solely a conscious choice to avoid pain. It's our brain's way of protecting us when the world feels like it's too much. After trauma, loss, or confusion, numbing is an emotional coping mechanism that enables us to continue going through the motions. It's how we survive. Once we are conscious of it, we can switch directions rather than continuing to do what's no longer serving us. Let the church say *ouch*.

The Point of Resistance

Choosing differently isn't an easy decision for everyone. Struggling doesn't make you weak, it makes you human. Sometimes, it's easier to remain in old patterns—the emotional chair—even if the solution is right in front of us. However, that protection, if held too long, becomes a cage we can't escape. The trick is knowing how to move from surviving to healing.

How to Resist the Temptation to Return

1. **Name the part of you that wants to give up.** What if you stopped denying that the desire exists and allowed it to be known?
2. **Check in with your body to see what you need.** Sometimes it's not giving up that you need. It's rest, replenishment, or a friendly connection. It's not failure to want to give up—it's your nervous system asking for a new way to be supported.
3. **Use soothing self-talk.** Try saying, "I can lack motivation to continue and take a break." Or "I'm finding this overwhelming and difficult, and that's normal, not a sign that I'm doing it wrong."
4. **Pause before deciding.** If you're overwhelmed, don't rush to fix, change, or overthink your situation. Waiting until the heaviest part of the emotional rain falls is okay. When you get a moment of reprieve, consider starting again.

You don't have to have it all figured out. I've never met a person who did. The unpopular wisdom is this: You don't have to become a new person. You're becoming someone with room for truth: your own, not someone else's timeline or image of "better." There's no need to strive for a perfect, neatly packaged version of healing. That doesn't exist. Instead, it's about being open to who you're becoming, including when the answers aren't apparent. Because the Truth Seeker Root, no matter how disruptive, always gives you the chance to release old wounds that shouldn't have been yours from the beginning. And that opportunity? That might be a risk worth taking.

Cultural Truths: New Roots in Old Dirt

Truth-telling isn't just personal—it's cultural. Similar to how the Shapeshifter Root grew to help us conform to our environments, we also took on "truths" about who we were and how those environments functioned. We are asked to keep secrets to protect reputations, swallow our pain to protect elders, or stay in broken systems to maintain status quo. But at what cost? When the Truth Seeker Root reveals the dysfunction in those systems, it challenges your personal comfort, yes, but also calls the entire ecosystem into question. Your healing might feel like rebellion to your community. Your grief might look like "being desperate for attention or playing the victim role." Naming manipulation might get you labeled as "too sensitive" or "disrespectful." The truth of who you are shines a light on the falsehoods and wounded areas of others. People don't welcome that, not with excitement anyway.

We inherently like the status quo because it brings certainty. We don't have to readapt. Anything or anyone who threatens that positions the community as needing to change. Change scares people because it's interwoven with uncertainty. For example, we see this with interfaith or interracial marriages: Families wonder, "Will the other person fit into our religion or culture? What if they don't pass on the family customs or distance our relatives from our traditions and beliefs systems?" It's less about who the person is marrying and more about what could happen if they don't "fall in line" with "the rest of us."

Your seeking out the truth isn't any different. When you start asking questions everyone understands not to ask, eyebrows lift. If you raise your children differently from how you were raised, others might have a lot to say. Or have to learn to readjust. For example, I visited my friend and she has a young daughter. I sat on the floor with her child, and we began making a castle. When she asked me how I got the blocks to stay, I jokingly responded, "It's a secret! I can't give away my best secrets."

My friend's daughter stood up on her two little feet, put one hand on her hip, and said, "In this house there are no secrets. We share with one other. We are allowed to give surprises, but only good ones. No secrets!"

I smiled and immediately made eye contact with her mom who said, "I taught her that. We're breaking that pattern. Too many family secrets in our culture have turned into trauma."

I told my friend I appreciated how she was raising her daughter; I agreed with sharing truths. I then commended her daughter for listening to her mommy and readjusted my language. "Well, no secrets. You're right. It's a bit like magic, and here's how I did it."

It's a small moment to show how I had to address my language in the household I was in. While I had intended on showing her how I built the castle, the way I joked and communicated needed to change. Ever since that interaction, I don't use that phrase in that way anymore. However, it could have been easy for me to say, "Oh, I was only joking. It's no big deal! When I was growing up, we all said, 'It's a secret.'" *Newness invites change, and it's for those on the receiving side to choose what to do with it.*

When Cultural Identity Evolves

Likewise, as you begin your healing journey, you might realize you grew up in a family that didn't express themselves openly or learned not to as they assimilated into a new one. A client experienced this after his older brother died. He said he wanted to "grieve what it was like not to have Big Bro around." He took more time off from the family business, got caught shedding a few tears, and talked about his sibling's death to strangers. His family wasn't thrilled about him telling people how their relative had died: "It's not good for business," they said to him. They also didn't understand his need for "all the off days."

"I grew up with immigrant parents who worked painfully hard to build something from nothing. They came to the States, didn't speak the language, and had no connections," he said to me. "They never took breaks and never complained. Me resting and taking days off feels like laziness to them. Sure, we all lost Haruki, but I'm the only one showing it."

Cultural dissonance causes distress, especially when grief is involved. You might feel proud of your lineage *and* deeply sad that your current expression feels foreign to it. You might carry a voice inside that says: "They survived so much—how dare I complain?" or "My feelings are small compared to what they went through." That's not disrespect. That's grief colliding with culture.

After validating how hard this is, and the overwhelm, I asked him, "What if your parents had to survive loss by not slowing down, and now, because of them—you don't have to grieve the same way? What if their silence and pushing through was their strength, and expression is yours?"

He stared at me for a moment. Then nodded. "I could see that. I can barely get through my days, and my life is easier. I guess they didn't have the choice to stop."

"Exactly," I said. "They plowed the ground so you could stand where you are. Your lineage planted the seeds. Your parents developed the fruit. Now you must protect the tree."

"Maybe that's generational progress," he sat up straighter and grounded his feet into the floor. "Honoring my brother's life and evolving how my culture grieves might be how I continue what my family built."

What my client was learning that day is in an identity reset; progress doesn't always look like doing more. It can be choosing to feel, to speak truth, and to sit with what's uncomfortable so the next generation doesn't have to. This is what generational healing looks like. It welcomes the Truth Seeker as a disruptor. Why? A root cannot stabilize the weight of the tree unless it breaks through the dirt that's already there. As I mentioned earlier, this tension is not evidence that you are failing. It's proof that you are expanding.

How to Honor Cultural Expansion

1. **Notice what your heritage gave you and how you're using it differently.**
   "They gave me survival. I'm using it to pursue peace."
   "They worked so I wouldn't have to hide. I'm learning how to be seen."

2. **Grieve what they couldn't give you.**
This is not to blame them, but to release the expectation that they could've taught you emotional fluency while they were fighting for basic survival.
3. **Remember that discomfort doesn't mean disloyalty.**
Being different from your family doesn't mean you're against them. It might mean you're what they hoped for and dreamed of, even if they're too conditioned by the past to recognize you as the answer.
4. **Courageously ask yourself the following:**
    - What truths did my culture or community teach me that was true in the past, but isn't applicable to my present and future?
    - What truths describe my life now, not then?
    - What known and unspoken rules am I breaking through? Can I name any benefits of dismantling them?
5. **Create a family tree of truths.**
Map out your known relatives or things that are known about your culture, people who look like you, your ethnicity, or background. Not all of us know where we come from or have information about our parents. Feel welcome to use what you have. Then ask yourself:

    - What beliefs and actions are normal in my community but are changing?
    - What beliefs or actions did my caretakers or parents hold?
    - What am I doing differently, or desire to?

This journey through the desert of unknowing isn't exile—it's initiation. You're not becoming someone new to abandon who you were, but to *integrate* what was once hidden. Healing is not a clean break from the past, it's a slow return to the parts of you lost along the way.

Friendly Recap

The Truth Seeker Root teaches us that clarity isn't always comforting—sometimes it unearths what we've buried to survive. In facing those truths, we begin to free ourselves from illusions that keep us small, silent, or stuck. This root doesn't demand perfection; it invites truth. Honesty is what allows identity to realign, rebuild, and root deeper.

Reflective Practice

Where am I still sleeping in the "emotional chair" instead of resting in the new truth I've created? What's the old pain I've normalized because it's familiar? What small act of trust could I try, even if it feels unfamiliar or wobbly?

Chapter 6

Is It Safe to Trust Myself?

I shouldn't have gone. My best friend called me up and invited me to her coworker's barbecue. I thought nothing of it. We were seventeen on summer break, and that meant being reckless and saying yes to things. Besides, she was a good friend, and I had nothing else to do. Why not go hang out for a few hours? I switched my outfit, sprayed on some perfume that said, "We grown *and* cute," then called her.

"Hey, girl, you ready?" she said, all bright and easy.

But before I could speak, my body clenched up with a high-tailed feeling: *Don't go. It's gonna be dangerous.* I scrunched my eyebrows and jolted my head. *Huh? Where'd that come from?*

"Ash? You there?" she said. "Girl, stop messin' around. Are you going or nah?"

"Yeah, I'll see you in a few, Tash." I put the phone down, stood in silence for a moment, then shrugged it off. I wasn't missing this for anything.

I left for the barbecue, and when we got there, that thing was dead. The cemetery had more life. There were about five or six guests, no music playing, and everyone was inside waiting for the night to start. *See? And I was going to say no!*

You could taste the burgers and ribs in the breeze going by, coolers were everywhere, and the grill flame was going. I walked over to the den and everyone waved. "Ash, these are my coworkers: Tina, Kasey, Mia, and Lisa. That's Mia's mom," Tasha said.

I smiled at everyone like a kid with peas on her plate—unenthused. Tasha caught it and side-eyed me. I knew I needed to lighten up, but I couldn't. Yes, everyone was cool, and the atmosphere was fine, but I felt off. I told them I was going to step outside for a minute. The sun beamed on my shoulders, and as I walked toward the driveway a chilling thought hit me: *Someone's gonna get shot.* I surveyed the place like an agent looking for clues. My hand involuntarily tapped my thigh. *What is going on?* As I was trying to figure it out, I heard a door open; it was Tasha coming outside.

"Hey, Ash!" she yelled. "You ready to go? Or you wanna hang?"

I wanted to tell her I was fine. It was cool, we could stay, but I couldn't. "Let's go. We can walk to my house or yours from here," I said. Now mind you, we were a whole town away. We had gotten a ride there and walking home wasn't exactly easy, but I was ready to leave.

"Say what? Girl, you crazy! It's ninety degrees in the middle of July. Walkin' where? I'm callin' my mama," Tasha said. "Hey, ma," she had her phone to her ear. "Ash and I are ready to go . . . what you say? Oh . . . I know we just got here, but we're ready to leave. Come get us!"

Her mama must've been on speed dial because she barely hung up the phone before our ride arrived. *There is a God.* We hopped in the car, and her mama said she never met two teens that didn't like barbecues. We got a good story about what it was like "back in her day," and I didn't mind listening. My body calmed down, and my soul felt good.

Before we knew it, we were at Tasha's house. We decided to stay in, eat, binge watch DVDs, and have ourselves a good time. Hours must've gone by, and when we got tired of movies, we turned on the regular TV to see the local news.

> BREAKING NEWS: A shooting has been reported tonight at a local barbecue gathering. According to witnesses, what started as a casual evening turned chaotic when two gunshots rang out—sending nearly a hundred teens, college students, and adults running for cover. The local police department has confirmed that one person was injured and another has died. Witnesses say an *unwanted and uninvited* individual appeared at the event shortly before the shooting began. Authorities are currently working to identify the suspect, and the investigation is ongoing.

"Oh my gosh, Ashley!!! Look! That's the barbecue we were at earlier! I'm glad we left! Where's my phone? I gotta call my coworkers!" Tasha said, running out the room.

I stared at the TV, listening to the reporter interviewing people who were at the barbecue. She walked to neighbors' houses and then showed where they predicted the shooting happened. I had stood in that spot. And I realized: The voice I almost ignored wasn't fear. It was *my inner wisdom*—and I didn't realize it. While I want to proudly say, see! I listened! That's only partly true. If it hadn't been for my friend asking "You wanna go?" I likely wouldn't have said anything. I didn't trust myself to act. I was lucky that my friend gave me permission to leave. What happened to me here isn't rare. In fact, it reflects a wider experience I see in countless people: We give our self-trust away to others and hope they choose the right decision for us.

Clarity Leasing

Trust doesn't disappear; it relocates. When we stop trusting ourselves, we hand it over: to a friend, a relative, a search on the internet. When we stop trusting people altogether, we trust in nothing. We say, "Nothing can hurt me," or "I don't trust in anything these days." But nothing can't hold you, grow you, or guide you. Nothingness is a void, and you'll never feel safe being held by emptiness.

Self-trust doesn't fail on its own. It gets stripped—either slowly or all at once—by people, systems, or circumstances that convince you your inner voice shouldn't be honored. Sometimes it's betrayal, like being dismissed after speaking your truth or watching someone say one thing and do another. Sometimes it's dismissiveness: caretakers who ignored your needs, praised you for compliance but not intuition, or punished you for being right too early. Sound familiar?

Over time, you learn to second-guess yourself, not because you're broken—but because it kept you safe. When the people around you prove untrustworthy, you begin to mistrust not only them, but your ability to choose the right people. Learning to trust again—yourself, others, even life—isn't a mindset. It's a rebuilding process, one that takes courage in the face of pain and fear.

Each of us is hard-wired to need and desire safety, and you'll likely continue to search for something or someone you can trust. You'll wait for signs, ask for permission, gather a consensus. We consciously call it being careful, cautious, or wise, and that might partly be true—but it is likely attached to fear and uncertainty.

Seeking out counsel and getting all the facts straight isn't a bad thing. I encourage it. You're likely better off doing so, assuming you're asking the right people and checking the correct sources. However, when people's opinions tug you in every direction—and every answer sounds like "good enough" or "maybe"—listen to the wisdom that's been speaking quietly the whole time. That voice matters most when people aren't there, when the facts aren't clear, and when no one can tell you, "This is the way."

There's a spiritual story of a messenger who was given a warning, not for himself but for a city of people. Without the message, the entire city would be destroyed. The problem was, he didn't like the city dwellers, so he chose to walk the other way, hop on a boat, and ask the sailors to take him to a town far from the city. As the ship sailed, suddenly a violent storm came, and the waves rose up toward the heavens. The crewmen threw over cargo and resources, hoping to lighten the boat.

As this was going on, the messenger was asleep, buried beneath the deck, as if none of the chaos above him existed. As the waves continued, the captain went looking for the messenger and, upon finding him, shouted, "How can you sleep right now? Get up! Call on your God! Maybe He will notice us, and we won't die." But the storm didn't calm. The sailors decided to cast lots—a spiritual practice used to reveal who was behind the chaos. And the lot? It fell on the messenger because he didn't deliver the warning.

The messenger decided to take responsibility for what he caused and instructed the men to throw him into the sea, but the men didn't listen. They continued rowing harder and doing everything in their might to get back to land. Eventually, after needlessly wasting valuable resources, cargo, and physical energy, the crewmen decided to throw the messenger into the waters and immediately, the storm ceased. The wind calmed, and the crew was saved.

This story appears in many ancient texts—the Torah, the Quran, and the Bible.[1] It teaches us that you can't outrun a storm that's already overtaken your boat—and you certainly can't calm it by ignoring where it began. Here's the deeper truth: Some storms rise from our own resistance, and others emerge when we abandon our own clarity. When we're grieving, overwhelmed, or navigating life transitions, it's tempting to lease our clarity to others—friends, mentors, strangers, and advanced technology. We hand them the wheel and hope they'll sail us somewhere safe. However, clarity that isn't yours can't permanently anchor you.

We build rafts from other people's opinions, only to find ourselves disappointed and regretful when consensus proves a poor vessel. You can't delegate discernment. Your Truth Seeker Root only answers to its rightful owner—you. Drift too far from your own wisdom, and you'll find yourself in storms you were never meant to sail.

Sometimes, we are like the sailors; we pour out time, energy, and emotional resources trying to save someone who was never ours to rescue. Discernment helps you see the difference—between those who truly need support and those who drain your strength while refusing to change. It reminds us that not every crisis is your calling, and not every person in the water wants to be pulled to shore.

[1] This story appears in multiple sacred texts, including the Book of Jonah (Tanakh/Old Testament) and Surah 37:139–148 (Quran). While details may differ, the heart of the story—a man running from what he was called to do—remains the same across faith traditions.

The Clarity Leasing Model

The crewmen were lucky to have their lives spared. I was fortunate to leave that barbecue before danger arrived.You've probably had moments like that—when a subtle instinct in your body registered something before your mind could explain it. Many of us override those signals because we've been conditioned to trust external reassurance over our own internal cues.

What our internal process of clarity leasing looks like:

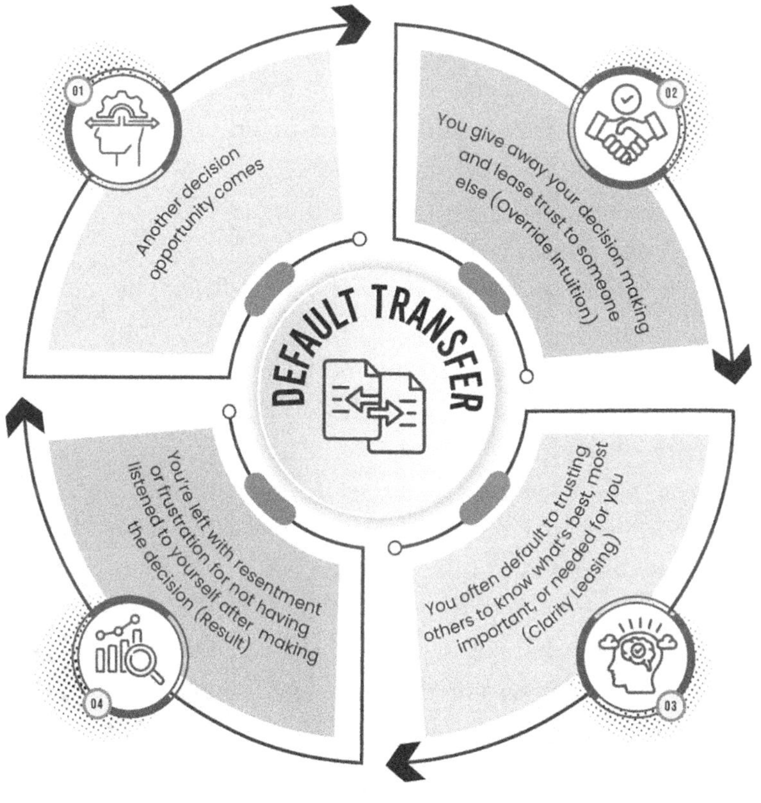

Think of this cycle as what occurs when you don't trust your sense of "what feels right." It doesn't start with the decision; it begins with your body.

1. *A choice shows up:* The moment arrives for you to decide upon something—be it a monumental decision, what's for lunch, or internal validation. Instead of feeling secure, an internal wobble occurs: Your body tightens, your stomach feels weird, your heart and breath changes its pace. An *I don't know* feeling hits you. That's your first cue.
2. *Instead of considering or reflecting, you seek to escape the discomfort of choosing:* Many people aren't aware they're doing this and if they are, how often. They look to others, constantly asking: What do you think? What would you do? Is this okay? Am I wrong for feeling/thinking/believing this? It feels easy to rely on others' decision-making process because in the moment, your nervous system wants relief, not responsibility.
3. *Giving your choice away becomes your default:* You believe others know what's best for you, or you can't choose until you've consulted them. Your body learns a "shortcut" to cope with indecision: avoid the discomfort → outsource clarity → get quick relief.
4. *Regret and resentment build while self-confidence decreases:* Your regret isn't dramatic, but it does sound like, "Ugh, I knew better. I should've gone with my first choice." You're frustrated with yourself and confused why you often end up here. Disappointment hits you not because you made the wrong decision, but because you didn't trust yourself to make the right one.

While it is okay to seek counsel from others, it's important that the loudest voice to confirm your life's choices is yours. Here's a quick guide to distinguish the two:

Seeking Wise Counsel Looks Like	**Clarity Leasing Looks Like**
You gather insight, information, and perspective.	You look for someone to tell you what to do or give you permission to avoid the discomfort of deciding.
You remain anchored in your identity, values, and intuition.	You disconnect from your own cues and override what your body or intuition already sensed.
Their input *informs* your decision, not replaces it.	Their opinion becomes the deciding factor, even when it doesn't feel right to you.
You hold the final say, and you feel at peace with what you've chosen.	You hand over the final say and later feel regret, resentment, or self-doubt because you abandoned your own knowing.

How to Dismantle Clarity Leasing

Patterns don't break with insight alone—they crumble through awareness, practice, and safety. Dismantling clarity leasing means giving your body and mind a new experience with choosing.

Here's how to do that.

Breaking Clarity Leasing

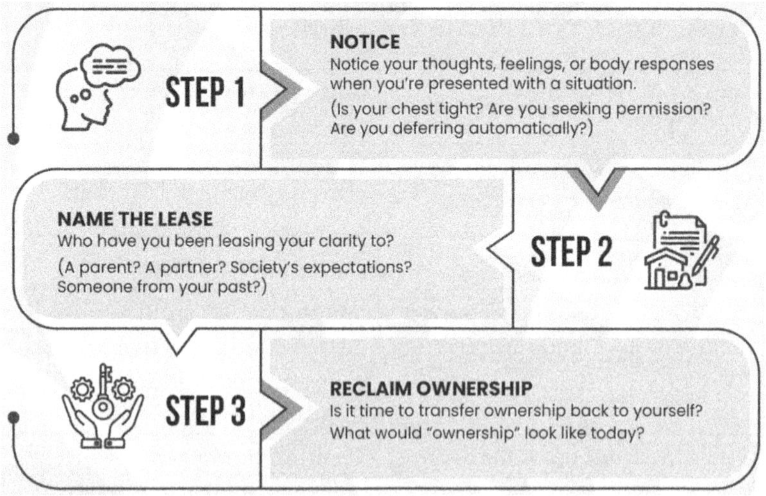

STEP 1: Notice

Most people lease clarity before they realize it's happening. The signal isn't in the thought—it's in your body.

When a decision comes toward you, pause long enough to notice:

- Does your jaw tense or teeth clench?
- Does your mind speed up or go blank?
- Do you feel the urge to ask someone what you "should" do?
- Do you feel small, unsure, or like you need permission?

These sensations aren't signs you can't decide. It's your body responding to the discomfort.

Practice #1: Before you act, breathe into the sensation for five seconds. Just stay with it. Let your body learn that the feeling isn't a threat—it's information. This simple pause interrupts the automatic transfer of your authority.

STEP 2: Name the Lease

Every lease has a history. A parent you didn't want to disappoint. A partner you depended on. A friend who always sounded more confident than you felt. A cultural script about who is "supposed" to know best. Maybe the fear of making another bad choice. Naming it out loud weakens its power. Try asking yourself:

- Whose voice do I hear in my head right now?
- Who am I hoping will approve this choice?
- What feeling am I trying to avoid by letting someone else decide?

When you name the lease, you stop the pattern from operating in the dark.

Practice #2: Notice if your body softens or tightens as you name the person or source. Your body already knows the truth—let it show you.

STEP 3: Reclaim Ownership (in Small, Safe Ways)

Ownership doesn't mean making perfect decisions. It means exercising the muscle of returning to yourself.

Ask:

- What do I sense about this?
- What outcome feels aligned with who I'm becoming?
- What would a small act of ownership look like today?

Ownership can be tiny:

- Choosing your meal.
- Picking the timing.
- Deciding your pace.
- Saying, "Let me think on that and get back to you."

As your body experiences decisions that don't lead to danger, the internal panic loosens. Remember, your mind and body inherently wants to have self-trust.

Practice #3: After you choose, give yourself a moment to notice what shifts inside you. It might be a hint of relief, a subtle settling, or simply awareness. What expands your capacity isn't making the "perfect" decision; it's allowing yourself to stay connected to your own voice, even when the outcome is uncomfortable or uncertain. Let your body register that choosing didn't disconnect you from yourself. That is the win.

> For ways to help build safety into your body, go to theidentityresetbook.com/extras.

What's Discernment?

Remember that the Truth Seeker Root is always living inside of you. It wants to guide you toward your inner truth, and to do that, it gives you discernment. Yet, how many times have you had the feeling of *don't go, don't trust them, don't say yes*, and bypassed it? Everything seems good, so we assume it is. That's why discernment is a critical skill to have: It distinguishes the right thing from the *almost* right thing. It's knowing fruit is rotten before you take it home and bite into it.

Seeing the difference isn't always easy though. Counterfeit money, designer clothing, "friends," and opportunities can look appealing. Add in experiences of loss, years of being conditioned by deception and manipulation, and recognizing the truth feels challenging. Is this your pain choosing for you, or your gut? Well, first you must understand what discernment is and isn't.

Discernment is the ability to choose what's true, right, and aligned beneath the surface of things. You might hear others define it as a sense of "good judgment." When we hear the word "judge" we might not always welcome it. This is especially true for people who struggle with receiving feedback, feel anxious about what others think of them, or are afraid of being misread. Struggling with these things doesn't mean something is wrong with you. In fact, it likely means there was a time in your life when you might have been unfairly labeled, criticized, and rejected. That said, having a sensitivity to the idea of "judgment" is normal and natural, but we're talking about a different type of inner clarity. True discernment comes with clarity and offers you peace. Below, I've outlined the difference between judgment and discernment.

Discernment	**Judgment**
Rooted in truth and love	Rooted in ego and fear
Seeks alignment with goodness	Seeks selfish personal preference
Leads to peace and clarity	Leads to anxiety and shame
Opens, explores	Assumes, blames, and concludes
Builds others up, including self	Tears down, isolates, or divides

Still, this is where things get hard. We're told catchy sayings that don't make room for nuance. We're taught:

Trust your gut.
Stick with the devil you know.
Energy doesn't lie.
If it's not a hell yes, it's a hell no.
Ghosting is okay.

What if your gut was trained on trauma and not truth? When survival mode becomes your baseline, your instincts aren't always wise; they are warnings built from past chaos. This is where discernment steps in. It's the voice of your Truth

Seeker Root, the part of you that asks not "What's familiar?" but "What's right?" What if "protecting your peace" is how you learned to avoid conflict you never had the tools to navigate? When you shut down or get defensive, it may not be because the person across from you is harmful—*it may be that your nervous system is confusing discomfort with danger.* That response, left unexamined, can unravel relationships that are genuinely safe, supportive, and healing.

If you're still navigating grief, you're not failing—you're learning new ways to live with what hurts. Growth often outpaces our coping skills long before our bodies stop bracing for harm that isn't there. As trauma language becomes mainstream, we've also seen an increase in casual mislabeling—calling someone bipolar or OCD when a licensed clinician would recognize that the criteria aren't met.

If we're honest, it's easy to treat every hurt as a red flag and every difficult person as a narcissist. But exhaustion and unrest can make even good people show up poorly—rude, withdrawn, reactive—not because they're disordered, but because they're depleted. Not every relational break is abuse, and not every mistake is toxicity. Sometimes distancing ourselves from others is a way to avoid parts of ourselves that need healing. Trauma often overprotects, warning us about danger that isn't there.

The nervous system doesn't ask, "Is this good for me?" It asks, "Have I been here before? Can I predict what happens next?" Based upon this, it formulates its thought patterns, actions, and habits. While traumatized minds make traumatized decisions, minds that are healing lean toward health.

When Instinct Gets Confused

If chaos was your normal, peace can feel threatening. This occurs with clients I've served in meditation and grounding practices. I had a client, Danielle, come screaming into a Zoom session that she was tired of everyone and wanted peace and quiet in her life. She said she was done dealing with her family and friends. I listened, then invited her to take a moment to be still and find a minute of calm in our space together.

Her face lit up, and she said, "That's what I need because I can't with their toxic behavior anymore!"

We softened into a few quiet breaths. I offered her the option to close her eyes or keep them open, whatever felt safest. About thirty seconds in, she shifted in her seat. Then again. Her jaw tightened.

"Is everything okay?" I asked her.

"Yes," she said, but her body disagreed. The worry showed before she could hide it.

"I'm wondering if you feel uncomfortable?"

"I don't like this."

"What feels off?" I asked.

"Being still." Her eyes got wider, and she looked at me with anger.

"Okay, let's resume our normal position for a moment," I said.

She sighed in relief and her face returned to its normal stance.

"I'm curious about what happened."

"I didn't feel still. It annoyed me and I felt like—" she stopped herself short, then spoke softly. "I felt like yelling."

We explored the difference between the *idea* of calm versus the felt experience of it. She realized that although she craved peace, the absence of turmoil made her uneasy. Somewhere along her journey she became accustomed to functioning well under havoc but unsure of how to ease into undisturbed moments.

At the next meeting, Danielle opened up by sharing an insight she gain since we had last met: "When my ex-husband and my kids tried talking to me, I'd start screaming at them. They'd say, 'Why are you always yelling at me? You're always angry.' Now I feel terrible. I realize I start arguments because calmness feels weird; I'm more familiar with chaos."

Bridging the Safety Gap

Your journey through truth will explain why distress is present. The next time you experience a moment of feeling unsettled, consider asking, "Why does this make me feel uncomfortable?" Know that the answer you receive might be unwelcome, too. Danielle let this inquiry vibrate within, and the truth wasn't one she wanted to embrace. It would have seemed easier if it was her family causing these problems because it was *theirs* to resolve. Knowing that she held part of the responsibility for the household's peace presented a different challenge: her need to change if she wanted to partake in harmony. This story is one example of a larger pattern. What she saw was the importance of discerning when she was in true danger—like when her mom stumbled into the house in the middle of the night after being at a bar—versus the family disagreements over misunderstandings.

Danielle thought peace meant silence. What she didn't realize was that her nervous system associated calm with danger. For her, stillness wasn't safety—it was exposure. When someone's trauma has taught them that chaos equals control, then anything slower, softer, quieter feels suspicious. I call this the **Safety Gap:** the emotional distance between what your soul wants and what your body believes it needs to survive.

- Your mind says, "I want healthy love," but your body says, "Where's the chaos I'm used to?"
- Your mouth says, "I want calm," but your stomach twists in silence.

Bridging the Safety Gap doesn't mean forcing yourself into immediate change. It means slowly retraining your body to recognize what's healthiest for you now and in the future. The more you practice this kind of self-reflection, the less you'll confuse your trauma's voice with your inner wisdom. That's why discernment isn't only a mental skill; it's a whole-body practice. Discernment safeguards you from others, *and* your unhealed self. Having the life that's closer to the one you want is possible. Your body only needs to earn your trust to receive it. And that distinction changes everything.

The Trauma-Calibrated Gut Test

Question	Gut Response	Trauma Response
Do I feel unsafe or just unfamiliar?	Pause and reflect	Withdraw or lash out
Is calmness suspicious or new?	Accept discomfort	Create chaos to feel control
Am I acting from now or from before?	Be present	Repeat patterns

Discernment in Action

Understanding discernment is one thing. Living it, especially when your nervous system is on high alert, is something else entirely. That's why discernment isn't just about having more information. It's about recognizing what kind of information matters where uncertainty, urgency, or emotional intensity exists. If knowledge is having the facts, and understanding is comprehending them, then discernment is knowing when, how, and why to act on them—or not. What does discernment look like in real life?

What the Truth Seeker Looks Like:

Situation	Wounded Instinct	Discerning Response
Someone withdraws after you express your feelings.	"I must've done something wrong. Let me fix it."	"I shared truthfully. Their reaction is not my responsibility."
You're offered an opportunity that feels exciting but rushed.	"Say yes now or lose it forever."	"Excitement is not the same as alignment. I can take a pause to consider it, seek counsel, or ask more questions about the opportunity."
A friend dismisses your troubles again.	"They didn't mean it. I'm being too sensitive."	"I need support, not dismissal. I might need to find someone else to share my loss with."
You feel nervous about ending a relationship.	"What if I'm wrong? What if it's not *that* bad?"	"I don't need more proof to leave something that hurts me."
You're meeting someone new or going on an interview.	"Do they like me? How do I get them to?"	"Do I like them? How do I feel about this person?"

Your Beliefs Will Cloud Your Discernment

Wounds are not your personality, but they will try to convince you they are. Over the last decade, I've witnessed this pattern across people from all walks of life: celebrities, blue-collar workers, those grieving a death, entrepreneurs, people navigating housing insecurity, and individuals raised in stable homes.

In the qualitative research I conducted while preparing this book, a pattern stood out: When life breaks you open, it's easy to start believing that what hurts you *is* who you are. The stories people told about themselves almost always started with loss and how it reshaped their sense of worth or identity.

This wasn't confined to the United States either. Forty-five percent of the people I interviewed were from other countries, and yet the themes stayed the same: It wasn't race, age, or location that shaped who they became after loss. It was the beliefs they carried underneath the pain. Dr. Caroline Myss, who studied this topic for fifteen years, calls this *woundology*: when we begin to identify with our emotional injuries and start relating to ourselves through them. This is where many people get "trapped," because our self-perception becomes tied to our self-protection—and that bond will either strengthen or weaken discernment.

Martha, a woman in her mid-thirties had recently relocated across the country. She decided to stop off in her hometown and felt disappointed when her best friend, Lucy, didn't make an effort to come see her.

"I told her I was going to be in town, and she never said, 'Hey, I'd love to meet up.'" As the details unfolded, I learned that the day before Martha's travels, she texted her friend a message: "Hey, I'm going to be in town for a few days. It'll be a quick trip, I'll only be there for two days and won't have time to see you, but it felt weird taking a flight out and not letting you know I was traveling."

When Martha finished reading the text, I looked at her and said, "It sounds like your friend honored your boundaries. Hearing the message, you told her you didn't have time to see her, and she respected that."

"She could have at least said, 'Hey, can you squeeze me in, or what do you mean you don't have time?' Like the saying goes, if they wanted to, they would."

"Is it possible that you wanted to see Lucy, but wrote the text otherwise?"

"Of course. Why wouldn't I have? If I asked her to meet up at the last minute, she might've said no. What's the point in asking her then if she didn't have time to prep for a meet-up?"

I sensed that beneath Martha's frustration with her friend was a wound of not being wanted. In many of our conversations, she mentioned being judged or rejected. By preemptively telling her friend she couldn't see her, she did what many who fear rejection do: I'll reject others before they have a chance to reject me. This can look like counting yourself out to avoid not being chosen, picking fights to justify disconnecting, or denying a desire to feel included. Now, it's important to clarify these actions aren't based upon a feeling, but rather a belief.

Here are what these feelings and beliefs sound like:

Stage	**What It Sounds Like**	**What It Represents**
1. Wound (raw feeling)	*"She didn't want to see me. That really hurt."*	Initial emotional pain from unmet need or loss
2. Wounded belief	*"I'm not important. That's why she didn't show up."*	Internalized story based on pain

Stage	What It Sounds Like	What It Represents
3. Reframe (healed belief)	*"I matter. This might have been a misunderstanding—not proof of my worth."*	Regained clarity and emotional safety
4. Healing feeling	*"I'm still disappointed we didn't connect. But I hope we can next time."*	Emotion held without identity collapse

Feelings are fleeting—they can be due to mood, hormones, circumstance, or stress. Beliefs are long held and built into our subconscious minds; they guide our decisions without consent. They shape what you expect from others, what you allow yourself to want, and how you interpret silence, perceived rejection, criticism, and care. Martha, like many others I've worked with, had a belief that said *I'm not wanted.* While we appreciate the ability to be self-protective, we can also understand how that becomes detrimental. It increases the chance of pushing away good people like Lucy, who respected her, while creating relationships that thrive off being "nice," having unvoiced needs, and "playing it safe." It's a strategy for "keeping my wounds untouched."

In your own life, maybe you've internalized beliefs that are tainting the life you want and how you wish to be seen by others. At the very least, your wounded beliefs prevent you from receiving the support needed to survive. Therefore, before you can act wisely, you must hear clearly. To do that, take a moment to notice your internal thoughts and outward behaviors. Slowing down is a trauma- and loss-healing act. It's saying, "I'm not who I was when I was forced to survive that moment. Now I get to choose differently." I've created the following chart to help you get started.

Fear Voice Says	Fear-Based Action	Discerning Action
If they loved me, they'd act differently.	Over-give, test their love, withdraw to see if they notice.	Ask for reassurance, state what you need.
I'm too much/ not enough/easily replaced.	Reject others to avoid rejection, avoid initiating.	Learn self-acceptance, give self-validation.
I feel unworthy.	Perfectionism, constantly saying "I'm sorry."	Celebrate wins, untie worth from performance.
I'm behind. Every-one else is doing better.	Constantly compare, delay launching ideas.	Define what success means for you.
If I open up, they'll abandon me, or I'll get discarded.	Constantly overthink, avoid closeness, put up walls.	Open up in safe ways, accept your feelings.

How to Detect the Truth Seeker Behind People's Motives

Discernment doesn't end with choosing who to tell what or who to have around. Your Truth Seeker Root stretches into nuance; it shows up when you think you know someone, only to realize you knew the version they practiced. *Truth is the difference between what their mouth says and what their heart whispers*. Most people mean well, but that doesn't mean they are well. Love can build a house with broken bricks—patching the cracks with good intentions yet leaving the structure vulnerable.

Good people—kind people, supportive people—can still steer you wrong. When you touch their scars, they react not to protect you, but to protect themselves. The old pain in them gets stirred by the new freedom in you. No one is exempt from this. In fact, the more intimate the relationship, the more certain it is that you'll press on something tender.

Sometimes it's subtle, like a parent's old pain triggered by their child's curiosity, not because the parent doesn't want to protect the child, but because that curiosity forces them to confront what they've hidden. A husband who struggles with voicing his needs resents his wife for voicing hers. A friend who is jealous of the abundance you have advises you from the scarcity wound in her soul. *What sits beneath this is an identity challenge.*

> *Some people struggle with telling you the truth because they can't tell it to themselves. The lies we tell ourselves are the hardest to untangle.*

Discernment goes beyond listening to what's said or watching what's shown. It's reading what's underneath with precision: the question behind the question, the part they didn't say, the tone that didn't match their words. My late fiancé used to say, "Honesty waits for the question. Transparency doesn't need one." Some people will only reveal what you ask for, while others—those who have embraced truth—will show you their heart without waiting for an invitation.

For many, being vulnerable means navigating a sea of self-doubt. When you've lost something (or someone) your emotional balance is fragile. You start questioning everything, including your worth. That makes you more open to outside influence, more susceptible to others' projections. Be careful who you listen to when you are vulnerable. When we are hurting, we seek out people who echo our pain, not encourage our growth or lessen our suffering. In the wrong hands, we'll exchange their validation as acceptance and approval for who we are, when instead, it can be opening the door to being treated in ways that wound us further.

Be Kind to All, and Accessible to Some

After loss or trauma, survivors tend to swing one of two ways: we either attach too quickly or not at all. Grief communities and mental health spaces are no exception. I've seen (and experienced) how we sometimes reveal everything to someone—just because they seemed safe, or because we were desperate to be heard. Trust should be earned, not assumed. You're allowed to pause before giving someone access to your story, your heart, or your energy. It's not rude. It's wise.

In *Gaslighting: Recognizing Manipulative and Emotionally Abusive People*, Dr. Stephanie Sarkis explains how manipulative people often "love-bomb" early in relationships—showering attention, praise, and intense connection before any real trust has been built. That's why it's vital to observe over time. Let yourself see:

1. **Mind:** Does expressing myself feel safe, or am I relieved to have a person to talk to?
2. **Heart:** Do I feel seen or dismissed when I offer vulnerability?
3. **Body:** What does my body feel like around them: tight, calm, nervous?

As a survivor of loss or hardship, it's important you don't confuse interest with intimacy. Someone offering you their attention doesn't mean they are safe to hold your truth.

Discernment protects what's sacred, not out of fear but wisdom. Let people reveal the patterns of who they are before you reveal the depth of your heart. You can be present, compassionate, and kind without handing someone the keys to your interior world. I've watched many trauma survivors overshare to gain bits of connection only to feel exposed in the end. Disorientation happens when being pursued is confused with being known. Discerning the difference between someone wanting access to you versus wanting a relationship with you protects your identity.

Imagine yourself as a delicate piece of clay that you've been shaping into something beautiful. It's still soft, still taking form. Now imagine that a friend asks to hold it before it's dry. They mean no harm, but when they take it from you, their fingerprints are impressed upon the clay. That's how easily someone can imprint themselves on your identity before it's solidified. What was once your truth can become distorted by someone else's perception, and when the clay hardens, it holds traces of their influence whether you wanted it to or not.

> *A true guide, someone who knows how to properly hold you, will help you shape your identity without affixing theirs upon you.*

Practicing discernment is:

- Not sharing your trauma story early on in a conversation or relationship.
- Pausing before trusting someone simply because they affirm you or relate to your pain.
- Realizing that some people are drawn to your light, but aren't equipped to hold your wounds.

Discerning What Influences Advice

People love giving advice. The fine print is this: Many speak from their vantage point—what they would do with their age, money, abilities, safety nets, relationships, or resources. Some project from limitation: fear, regret, insecurity, or old wounds. Others speak from advantage: more savings, fewer responsibilities, better health, greater freedom, or a different stage of life. They imagine, "If I were you, here's what I'd do," without realizing they're describing what someone in *their* position could do—not what's appropriate, attainable, or wise for others. That's why your job is to discern the source of their advice. It looks like this:

- A parent who attempts to fulfill their lost dreams though you.
- The person who's never experienced grief advising you how to feel.
- People who've never started a business telling you how to run a successful one.
- Someone advising you to push harder or "do it all" because they're speaking from a level of physical or emotional capacity you don't have.
- A friend in a different life stage urging you to "start over," forgetting they have freedoms, time, or support systems you don't.

Their words might sound wise, and their tone might be confident, but that doesn't make it true for *you*. Remember that discernment is accessing the right thing from the almost right thing; it's seeing behind what's presented. Becoming interested in what motivates a person's answer allows you to gain clarity on where it's coming from and where it's going. Sometimes, the wiser move is to trust yourself—even imperfectly—than to follow someone whose advice would lead you further from what's best.

You've likely heard people say, "If you didn't learn what to do, you've learned what not to do!" That sounds good, until you realize you'd be better off having learned the correct thing first. Growing up in a household where everyone communicated through yelling and belittling another might teach you how not to speak to people. It doesn't teach you how to be assertive, give encouragement, and respond effectively. Watching people run from problems might teach you to avoid confrontation, but it won't teach you how to face hard truths. Knowing what not to do is not the same as knowing what to do. Healing means learning the difference.

How to "Check the Root" of Someone's Advice

You make wise decisions by asking wise questions. Before internalizing someone's opinion or advice, ask:

1. **Is this advice based on my reality or their experience?**
    - Did they ask about my needs, values, or situation, or are they assuming based on their own?
    - Does it make sense for my life?
2. **Does their life reflect the outcome I want?**
    - Have they made wise choices in this area, or are they guiding me from regret, hindsight, or failure?
    - Are they telling me what to do without any guidance of how to do it?
3. **What do I feel in my body when I hear this advice?**
    - Do I feel empowered, seen, and calm, or guilty, small, and confused?

- Is my body sensing that there's something in it for them if I follow this advice?

4. **What fearful or encouraging language are they using?**
   - Are they warning me out of love or out of fear?
   - What exactly are they afraid of, and does that fear belong to me?
5. **Do they speak with a sense of longing?**
   - Is this person trying to vicariously live through me?
   - If applicable: Are they willing to learn alongside me?

Friendly Recap

Discernment isn't limited to choosing right from wrong. It's knowing yourself so intimately that you can tell what applies to you and what doesn't. Grief and hardship shake that sense. It makes you question what's real. As your roots deepen, your discernment sharpens, and your identity becomes grounded.

Let intuition be your compass and allow discernment to light the way. You'll see your life and the people in it with clarity and stop living from desperation and fear. You'll possess the ability to choose relationships that *support* you, not demand a lesser version of you. Discernment teaches us that life without safety isn't freedom, it's survival. Let it be your quiet strength, guiding you to move wisely, trust appropriately, and listen deeper. The Truth Seeker Root produces the fruit of internal validation and rest. It's yours for the harvest.

Pick one area of discernment from this chapter, then put it into practice. Know that you don't have to apply everything at once in every aspect of your life. If you improve one thing, you're still making progress.

Root Three

THE RELEASER

The Dragon Within Us

I was on my normal commute to college and listening to the radio when the interviewee said, "Pain is a treasure, locked in a dungeon, guarded by a dragon." Although that was years ago, and I wish I remembered who said it, the imagery stayed with me. However, throughout the years the metaphor evolved as I did. I began telling myself, "*Identity* is the treasure, locked in the dungeon, and guarded by a dragon."

Reproduced with permission from Sutan Griansyah / Ashley Ormon

The interviewee had a more traditional take in that we need to "slay the dragon"; my perspective differs. Not every dragon should be slain. Some appeared to protect you when no one else did and killing it isn't necessary because it kept you alive. You can thank it for doing so, release it after, and let it fly home.

Doing this shows you how to build capacity. For true release isn't having power *over* something, it's having peace *with* it. A king or queen who has peace among their people is respected over those who seek war and control.

Chances are, you've fought many battles by now and don't need another one. Having a dragon represents the internal fears, wounds, and unhealed stories you carry. It's your past pain that has shaped your present actions. It's the thoughts and behaviors that keep you looping—even when you're actively seeking a way out. Sometimes, the other shoe that drops is the trauma that never got dropped. Woefully, many of us never free the dragon within, and thereby tap into our treasure, because we fear what doing so may cause. Anxiety arrests us and keeps us tied to psychological unrest. True rest is found in asking the dragon what is being guarded, what you need to be nurtured, and if you are willing to be free.

What stands between the life you have and the life you want? Is it the fear of failure? An old story of inadequacy? Maybe it's the thought of who will stay and who will leave should you decide to take on the task.

This is when the Releaser Root shows up. It wants to dig deep into the dungeon of our lives, grab hold of the dragon, and free it. The dragon, frustrated by unmet needs, rebels. It takes control over our lives, and it creates an escape plan in endless forms: distraction, aggression, ego, running away, overthinking, caretaking, needing control (or giving it all away), people-pleasing—and sometimes drugs, sex, or alcohol—all to become free. What most call dysfunction are the wounds of a dragon, trapped inside the painful dungeon of its experiences, and seeking a way out.

The Dragon of Grief

For many of us, leaving the past behind feels impossible. You've named your dragon "Grief," "Trauma," or "Loss," and no matter how much you wish you could undo what's been done, the pain stays. When these wounds write your story, it feels like each chapter is written in the ink of hurt and regret.

But the dragon isn't the pain; it's the fear of confronting it—the part of you that hesitates to face the wounds you've kept buried for so long. The real struggle isn't only in confronting the bad things that have happened; it's also your beliefs attached to them. This is where the work begins. As you journey through, you'll notice your roots interacting with one another.

The Shapeshifter says:

"Don't face the dragon. If you do, everything will fall apart. Continue reshaping."

The Truth Seeker says:

"Look again. This isn't the hardship or grief; it's the fear you've built around it."

The Releaser says:

"You can be safe now. Let's free the dragon and enjoy the treasure behind it."

Healing does not mean erasing. Healing transforms the wounds we carry to make us more whole and stable. Grief invites you to release the dragon—that wounded story that screams underneath. Life's paradox is that the creature you've been most terrified to understand holds the keys to healing. When you greet the dragon, it soothes itself knowing its truly seen and fully loved.

If the Truth Seeker Root teaches you how to discern what's true, the Releaser Root teaches you how to soften what's gripping your soul. As the root that listens, it doesn't demand you rip out the past by force—it honors what the past gave you. Then, with timing and tenderness, it invites you to let it go.

The Releaser Root

What's holding you back may have once held you together. That's why it's not about moving on; it's about moving *differently*. Release is not forgetting, it's unfastening. It's removing the idea to "heal beautifully" and have a "testimony" before the bleeding is over. Society wants your uprising after the downfall to come with a public relations campaign of "how you made it out" and "you're not what you've been through." What we don't see is the behind-the-scenes before people get there, and it looks like sacred chaos—which no one aspires to.

The Releaser Root works on willingness and opportunity: Would you let go if you had the chance? Snatching away what you're holding doesn't breed trust; it breeds more distress. The soft invitation to release means:

- Shedding the roles you were forced into
- Giving back what others projected onto you
- Unlearning your emotional impersonations

- Letting go of an identity fueled by suffering
- Releasing coping strategies that harm you and others

Please understand that release isn't a one-time event in the beginning. It's a chosen practice. Holding on is a reflex we adopted, and operating opposite of that won't feel natural at first. We have to make peace with the fears we've kept in the dungeon. There will be moments you might wonder, "Did I do the right thing?" Your relationship with self-doubt and confidence will dance awkwardly at first until one learns to follow the other's lead. That's why we don't start by cutting things off. We start by unraveling the Shapeshifter Root from the Releaser Root. That means acknowledging that release:

Is not betrayal.

- You're not dishonoring your past by choosing your future.

Is not perfection.

- Your release doesn't need to be visible, impressive, or measured.

Is not emotional amnesia.

- You're allowed to remember without being required to relive.

Is not an act of punishment.

- Letting go isn't the consequence of wrongdoing but of releasing what isn't beneficial.

Is not spiritual bypassing.

- You don't get to skip your suffering by pretending it no longer hurts.

Is not disconnection.

- Release doesn't harden you. It softens you and allows for deeper connection.

Reframing the process as open palms rather than clenched fists makes room for heavy things to pass and good ones to land tenderly. Above all, this root releases the overwhelm you've been feeling by removing what survival required: crying tears that were never yours to feel but handed to you anyway.

The beauty in this is that full trust isn't needed, which is helpful if you're still working on this area. Some schools of thought insist that healing begins only when a person feels safe. But what I've seen—in clients, in grief, and in hardship—is that healing commences with something smaller than safety. It begins with a touch of *micro-readiness*. A moment where, despite fear, we say: *I'm open, I'm interested enough to see what this is about.* The Releaser Root doesn't arrive with fanfare. It finds us in the pause between exhaustion and surrender. It roots itself when there's the smallest crack between fear and possibility—and asks nothing more than our *willingness*.

You don't need to force detachment, forgiveness, or transformation. You don't even need to believe it's possible yet. Willingness—not certainty or hope—is how healing begins. Allow the Releaser Root to begin its sacred work of pruning. Sense it kneeling beside you, removing each weight your soul has carried. In the stillness, hear it say, "Let's place these burdens down *together*."

Chapter 7

The Dangers We Feel in Releasing

Few people talk about the grief that comes *after* grief. Discernment and truth kick in, and you realize how much you tolerated and what you deserved instead. We grieve the version of ourselves that smiled, that shoved down anger into a tiny square hole. We grieve not because we want to reexperience it; we grieve because we see how much we had to carry while making it through.

And when you begin to really see, when clarity floods in, you don't only notice what hurt you. You see what was buried underneath. Knowing there's treasure behind the dragon is one thing. Understanding you almost didn't make it, while carrying gold between your ribs, is another.

Releasing the old brings relief and joy; it's the ability to breathe again (or for the first time). But for many people, letting go creates waves of sorrow—or at best, nostalgia. It's like outgrowing your first house and buying a new one, no longer fitting into your skinny girl jeans after having a child, or getting rid of the car you loved. The next house might be bigger, the new jeans look just as good, and your new ride has all the bells and whistles with low mileage. *But man*, you made some memories in those things.

You start thinking about how you raised a family there, how the car transported your loved one before they died. You recall, what feels like not so long ago, how that outfit was worn at your graduation, the first date, or that time you had a moment to yourself. Letting go of *some* things often means letting go of *each* thing held within them. That's why you might even miss the "bad" moments—because if you're honest, those were fun too. Sure, you wouldn't get involved in that stuff now, but back then, it was great. You reminisce, and you find yourself saying, "Those were the good ol' days. Times were hard, but at least we had each other."

Releasing old versions of you—what you thought was true, what was true then but isn't now, the aspects of life you held close—works the same. We get sentimental. Letting go comes with more tears and heartbreak than you anticipated. That isn't a sign you've done it wrong, and it isn't the universe telling you to stop here and go back. It's you being human. You're allowed to miss what wasn't supportive and healthy. That's normal. The shapeshifter life wasn't all bad, but truth be told, it wasn't all good either.

The Ache of Good-bye

How do you grieve a good thing that hurt you? The friendships that felt like family but faded when you hit rock bottom. The people who changed once you finally made it to the top. The marriage that was beautiful until it wasn't. The heartbreak of doing such a good job that your children are now strong enough to leave home. The long hours you poured into a career that left your body aching. The relationship that meant everything—now buried in a casket—leaving a wound in your heart that no therapy, remedy, or prayer will fully close. How do you grieve a good thing that hurt you?

Culture teaches us that not having closure is closure. But if that were true, we'd all be at peace.

The opposite of closure isn't resolve—it's acceptance.

And that's a hard thing to contend with. Not because there aren't more facts to find, more questions to ask, more prayers to pray. There usually are. *Acceptance isn't about the absence of options, it's about no longer chasing them.* It's releasing the need to dig, to uncover, to make sense of what refuses to explain itself. It's letting go of what's not there—the illusions, the what-could-have-beens—and being still with what is.

Acceptance is the realization that what you're doing is no longer working. That peace, should it ever come, won't arrive by circling the same path. It comes from facing the discomfort of what's no longer there. It's the decision to stop searching for more answers—why they died, how they died—and begin learning how to live with the ache of them not being here at all. It's the quiet breaking of illusions—of who you thought they were, who you hoped they'd become, and the potential you believed was still within them.

You can search forever, but in the end, the answers aren't going to return the things you've lost. No amount of searching will undo the choices you didn't get to make, the moments you didn't get to share. It's the final, heartbreaking realization that some things have to remain untold, unexplainable. Acceptance is looking at the situation and saying, sometimes painfully so, *These are the facts. I cannot change them.*

Acceptance is hard because it asks us to release something. It requires us to let go of what we always wanted to hold onto—what felt like it belonged to us, what we believed we were worthy of receiving. It asks us to grieve what may never arrive. It's a bittersweet good-bye, because we release the looping—the going over and over again, trying to make sense of what cannot be made sense of. It's recognizing that even if we *did* understand the why, the how, the what, and the when—it likely wouldn't make us feel any better. We'd still find ourselves back at the beginning, searching for a different outcome.

Acceptance says: *I can't fix this. And I don't like how powerless it makes me feel.* It's the memory we reach for when the ache returns. It's the broken dreams we set down when it gets too heavy to carry forward. Acceptance shifts the mind and body but rarely reality itself. That's the strange thing about releasing. It gives you the relief you asked for by taking what gets left behind: people, hope, dreams, wishes, homes, potential, health. Maybe that's why we reminisce and recount the good before the crisis ever hits, because we realize one of the hardest truths of all: Sometimes the things we hold onto are more painful to release than they are to carry. Releasing what felt good doesn't feel good once it's gone.

Maybe You're Not Avoidant, You're Afraid

Avoidance seems like a best friend in moments we decline to accept what's in front of us. It has many faces—emotionally, mentally, and physically. Avoidance can look like putting distance between yourself and someone or something. Mentally, it shows up as indecisiveness, creating illusions or fantasies, or pushing away thoughts that require your attention. Emotionally, it shows up as withdrawing from situations or people that stir discomfort in you or filling your days with distractions—of which there are no shortage these days.

It's common for those on the outside to feel frustrated with those who avoid what seems "obvious" and "needing attention." And to be fair, they may have valid reasons for their frustration. What isn't obvious is that people don't avoid emotions and circumstances because they're unwilling—they avoid them because they're afraid. They fear that if they face the conflict, the pain, the grief, or the decision in front of them, it will be too much to bear. Acceptance feels like too much to hold. And so, avoidance seems like the easier, safer choice.

Imagine you haven't had anything to drink all day and you're thirsty. I tell you that if you go into the family room, there's a stockpile of cold water waiting for you. To me, the answer seems obvious: Go inside and grab the water bottle. But maybe for you, you remember that the last time you walked into that room, a dog was inside and he bit you. You ran out bleeding, hurt, and afraid. You'd be far less enthusiastic about stepping back inside. Instead, you might tell yourself, *I'm not that thirsty right now. I can wait.* You might even distract yourself every time your body cries out for hydration.

Now imagine if I told you: "There's water in the family room. The dog is still there. When you walk in and he comes up to you, say, 'Hey boy,' and gently rub his head. Then grab the water." You might ease up a bit. Maybe you'd think, *Okay, before I get too dehydrated, I'll give it a try.* And if I told you, "I'll go with you to get the water," you might even feel safe enough to open the door.

You'd watch me walk in, see the dog rush toward us, watch me greet him and rub his head, then grab two bottles of water. And the next time you came over thirsty, you might feel less avoidant—if at all. Why? Because now, you're equipped to face the thing you feared. You know how to tame the animal inside. Avoidance often works the same way. You fear the possibility of being overtaken because you're not confident you can manage the situation.

Feeling Isn't Safe

We were walking along the Long Island Sound barefoot, which sounds lovely until you realize the North Shore of Long Island is filled with rocks and stones. It seemed appropriate though. The beach was my happy place, and I had met up with my friend, Lauren, after having a huge argument with my then-boyfriend.

"I can't believe you did that," Lauren said to me. "You said what to him? It's like you don't have any heart at all. How do you love someone and do that?"

I felt my body tighten, and I hung my head low. She wasn't being mean; she was being honest. I had recalled the events of what happened the day before, the circumstances, and how I acted. It looked like everything but love. I kept walking and didn't give her an answer.

"Even now," she said, with her hair being carried in the breeze, "You look so frozen, so cold. Why are you so—so—*emotionless*."

There it was. Those words again. I had been called cold and emotionless more times than I heard my own name. While most knew me as kind and caring, others such as a former boss at work, friends, and people close to me said I lacked empathy, or else was inconsiderate. But inside? I felt heartbroken and defective. I had pages upon pages of journals expressing my emotions. If the stars represented them, my internal language was infinite. Yet, when it came to outwardly expressing how I felt, I looked like freshly dried concrete: I was hard as a rock. There were no cracks to get in, and surely nothing was extending out.

"Are you okay with being this way?!" Lauren said to me. Her eyebrows scrunched up and her voice got louder. While I *knew* she wasn't yelling at me, I *felt* like she was. My heart and my mind processes weren't congruent. *I'm ashamed. I'm a bad person.*

I finally answered her. "I'm not cold. I feel a lot of things."

"Things isn't a feeling."

That's what he told me too. My heart sunk.

"Why don't you say how you feel then. You realize being this quiet isn't normal, right?"

"I don't know how," I told her. "It's hard for me."

"You need therapy."

"I want to go. I've been wanting to go. I'm pretty sure there's a bunch of stuff messed up with me because of the way I grew up," I told her. "But I still live with my parents. I'm afraid if I go to therapy, and start feeling and getting better, it's gonna make it harder to live at home. I have one year of college left. I'll move, then get help."

Lauren pulled off her backpack and dropped it in the sand. She took out a piece of paper to write something. When she was done, she yanked the sheet from her notebook and handed it to me.

I cautiously grabbed it. *Christian therapist*, it read, with a phone number beneath it.

A Christian therapist?—hell no. (Can you use that in the same sentence?) "No thanks, I told her. I grew up in a religious home as it is. I don't need someone telling me 'it's the devil.' Sometimes it's just us—our selfishness, bad habits, patterns, and stubbornness," I said.

"Girl, you don't know a thing about therapy, do you? That's the therapist I go to. She's good and she's helped me out."

Eh, has she? I thought. But I kept that one to myself. "Thanks." I told her.

"But back to your relationship. Why are you with him if you can't open up?"

I didn't answer her question, and I could tell she got tired of being ignored. We walked most of the remaining shoreline in silence. I replayed her question in my mind, and images of my childhood appeared. I thought about all the times I told my family I was sad, only to be told I was "being too dramatic." I recalled all the moments I said I didn't want to live and was told, "You just want attention." I didn't have a term for it then, but I was struggling with suicidal ideation. With each step on those hard rocks, my mind replayed moment after moment where I was vulnerable, open, expressive. More times than not, I was dismissed, discarded, or mocked. It wasn't that I didn't want to accept how I felt—I learned it was safer not to. And it would take years of undoing, and having experiences with people who held me safely, to bring healing.

Why We Resist

It was easy for my friend Lauren to assume that I was cold and unfeeling. Perhaps, on the outside, I was. But not because I chose or wanted to be. It was the result of an emotional vow I had made: *Never again will I let my vulnerability be weaponized.*

The trauma bargain became simple: *If I numb myself and stay expressionless, I'll remain safe.* What we don't always realize is the cost of the bargain—not only to ourselves, but to others. The cost of not being able to express what we feel. The cost of struggling to build healthy relationships. The cost of unintentionally wounding the very people we want to be close to.

I had seen that cost in my own life. Keeping my walls up, shutting down, avoiding openness—it hurt the relationship I was in then. Being the victim in need of protection made me a villain in defense. I unintentionally hurt others who wanted to love me but couldn't reach what I kept guarded. It's the hidden cost of unsupportive self-protection: *Hurt people really do hurt people.*

Freedom doesn't feel free when it threatens our present-day safety. If identity is a treasure, locked in a dungeon and guarded by a wounded dragon, then what I needed wasn't just the courage to enter—I needed reassurance that releasing the dragon wouldn't leave me burned. It was never the treasure I feared. It was being overtaken by the wounds guarding it. The Releaser Root isn't solely about letting go. It's about what happens when we finally dare to do it. We often assume that if someone wants freedom badly enough, they'll change. We hear it all the time: "If they wanted to, they would."

That sounds reasonable for those who have the emotional capacity, internal development, mental skill set, and psychological maturity to tolerate what might surface. For those who feel confident that, whatever comes next, they have the support—internally, if not also externally—to face it. How often do we meet someone who checks *all* those boxes? Not often.

For those who have experienced things like profound loss, hardship, life transitions, and health challenges, release rarely comes neatly packaged. It feels like yet another demand on our already pressured lives. It requires us to step into wide open spaces without knowing who we'll be on the other side. That doesn't feel like safety. It feels like exposure. Standing between us and that freedom is the dog carrying our fears: the woundings we didn't cause but received anyway. It's easier to stay outside than try to pat the animal on the head to get by. So we settle for, "This is who I am. This is how life is," instead.

Survival isn't designed for growth—it's designed for preservation. When you're just trying to make it through, there's little energy left for self-reflection, healing, or release. You're not thinking about becoming—you're thinking about enduring. That's why so many people stay locked in roles, identities, and patterns long after they've outgrown them, not because they lack the desire to change, but because change requires safety. And safety often feels like a privilege that survival doesn't offer. Unfortunately, there's only one way out of this. When life changes, we are forced to change. If we don't change to improve our lives, we risk morphing into someone unfavorable.

Ways We Enter Unsupportive Change

When we avoid release, we don't pause change—we redirect it. The longer we postpone release, the more our nervous system tries to compensate, shapeshifting us in ways that feel safer in the moment but become costlier over time.

As physician and trauma expert Dr. Gabor Maté teaches, emotions are designed to metabolize what is healthy and reject what is not—much like the immune system does. But when emotions like anger are suppressed, the immune system can become suppressed as well. Unaddressed trauma doesn't remain neutral inside us—it gets stored, often showing up not only in our behaviors but also in our bodies.

Research continues to show that chronic emotional stress can dysregulate the immune system, contributing to inflammation, cardiovascular disease, autoimmune flares, and long-term physical vulnerability.[1] Suppressed emotions fuel patterns that reach far beyond our choices, impacting how we live, how we heal, and how we carry what remains unresolved. There are four ways this can happen: resigning hope, putting ourselves last, clinging to anger, and isolating or withdrawing.

Resigning Hope

At some point, release can feel too risky—especially after grief or trauma has weighed on us for so long. It's not that we don't care or that we've stopped hoping altogether; it's that imagining something different starts to feel too exhausting, too vulnerable, or too painful to even attempt. And so, whether consciously or subconsciously, we decide that it's easier, safer, and even more protective to stay where we are.

While this can look like acceptance, it isn't. As Dr. Russ Harris explains, it's pseudo-acceptance—"using a so-called 'acceptance technique' with the hope it will make unwanted thoughts, feelings, [and situations] go away."[2] In other words, it looks like tolerance. We might not release the old or decide to alter how we are, but we aren't satisfied either. It's the difference between feeling accepted and feeling tolerated. And deep down, we long to be received.

Over time, resignation quietly reshapes who we believe ourselves to be. Grief and trauma start to feel less like experiences we've lived through and more like definitions of who

---

[1] Alotiby, A. (2024). Immunology of stress: a review article. *Journal of Clinical Medicine* 13 (21): 6394. https://doi.org/10.3390/jcm13216394.

[2] Harris, *Trauma-Focused ACT*, 150.

we are. The longer we stay here, the more loss fuses itself to our identity because sometimes it hurts less to believe that nothing new is possible than to risk hoping again. Resignation sounds like:

- "Nothing I'm doing is working—I guess I just have to accept it."
- "It is what it is."
- "I should just be happy with what I have."
- "This is my life now."
- "Nothing's likely going to get better, so what's the point?"
- "Maybe I need to lower my expectations. It's not meant for me."

The Releaser Root acknowledges all these things, while giving you the opportunity to experience life beyond what feels like being defeated. It creates space to say, maybe this is my life right now, but it doesn't always have to be. What if I don't settle for being content with what little is left and allow myself to have something more? Maybe you don't have to move on. Maybe you can move differently with what remains. The Releaser Root honors the version of you that kept going and invites you to consider who you could be when survival isn't leading the way.

Putting Ourselves Last

In our deepest moments of self-sacrifice, we may believe that if we carry everyone else's burdens, it will somehow make us more loved or accepted. Often, we sacrifice our own needs, desires, and identity for the comfort, happiness, or stability of others. Martyrdom says: *If I can't release it, I'll carry it all to keep the peace.* It convinces us that suppressing what's true inside us is somehow noble when really, it slowly erodes both our sense of self and the very relationships we're trying to protect. This is like saying "happy wife, happy life," rather than "happy spouse, happy house," where both people invest in the welfare of themselves and their partner.

We tell ourselves that if others are content, our sacrifice is justified. But self-betrayal isn't love. It's a form of survival that trades authenticity for proximity and acceptance for quiet tolerance. Martyrdom keeps the Shapeshifter alive by holding the weight of unspoken truths so that we can belong where we've always been, even if it costs us who we are. Identity Martyrdom can sound like:

- "At least I did a good job."
- "It's fine, I'll be okay as long as everyone else is."
- "Everyone depends on me and expects me to do it."
- "They've been through so much. I can't add my problems to the mix."

There's grief inside martyrdom, and its ache goes unnoticed and unspoken. Sometimes the grief sounds like: *I wish I could be accepted for who I am. I wish someone would really see me. No one hears or understands me. I want to be held. I wish I had someone who poured into me the way I pour into everyone else.* Sacrificing the essence of who we are for the sake of others leaves us longing for reciprocation.

It's okay to want to be chosen, nurtured, and loved without needing to carry everything first—or always. Releasing identity martyrdom provides the chance to experience this. More importantly, releasing goes beyond people finally seeing you. It extends to you finally seeing yourself—and as someone who is worthy of love, belonging, and rest.

Clinging to Anger

Anger and frustration can be natural responses when healing seems out of reach. We push against what we can't control because protecting our hearts feels safer than exposing them. It's okay to get angry when life feels unjust, and rebellion can be a form of emotional protection.

When healing feels unreachable, some of us turn our pain into armor. If we can't become who we truly are, we absorb the villain—resenting others for living what we feel unable to access within ourselves. Bitterness and resentment take up jobs at the identity desk, not only shielding us from vulnerability, but protecting us from the ache of what feels permanently out of reach.

Sometimes rebellion looks like jealousy: *I resent you for being who I'm not.* Or: *I reject the parts of you I struggle to accept within myself.* We push away the wounds we see in others because they expose the unhealed wounds in us. Rebellion becomes a way of protecting ourselves from ourselves—guarding what we haven't yet been able to hold, grieve, or make peace with.

On the outside, rebellion looks like confidence or strength—like we've risen above the people or situations that hurt us. Underneath, it's grief reshaped into cynicism. We try to outrun the ache by hardening against it. If resignation tolerates pain, and martyrdom absorbs it, rebellion spits it back with fire. It sounds like:

- "I don't need anyone—I'm better off on my own."
- "Why should they have it so easy?"
- "I'll pull away before they get the chance to hurt me."
- "They wouldn't survive half of what I've had to carry."
- "I can't be around people like that—it stirs up things I don't want to deal with."
- "Their struggles hit too close to home—I'd rather not go there."

If you've experienced trauma, you might rebel against the idea that you "should" be okay, that life "should" go on as normal. There's a reactionary quality to this, especially for those who are neurodivergent, who may feel like they're constantly fighting against the world's expectations and definitions of what it means to be "good" or "normal."

Rebellion doesn't always have to be destructive. Sometimes we need to push back to find space for healing before we can consider letting our guard down. It acts as a moment of self-assertion, a refusal to accept things the way they are. Still, it's important to ask: What am I protecting, and what might I be missing out on by keeping everyone at arm's length?

Isolating or Withdrawing

Animals tend to withdraw in the days leading up to their death. They turn inward, sometimes hide, to protect themselves when they feel weak. It also helps them conserve the limited energy they have left. Metaphorically, people can have the same tendencies when who they are seems to be dying on the inside. Experiencing long periods of rejection, being shamed, and being unseen can naturally lead anyone to thinking, "If they don't see me for who I am, then they won't notice if I'm invisible."

It can feel extremely soothing to pull away from others, including the people you love, as a form of safeguarding the aspects of you that remain. It feels safer to fade out before anyone has a chance to misunderstand you again. Disconnecting in this way over time can become an unsupportive form of control. You tell yourself you're "protecting your mental health," or "matching their energy," when really, you're protecting your pain. Rest assured, cushioning your pain isn't a bad thing. However, it might not be the best thing to create the peace you long for.

Prolonged withdrawal creates incongruency: We want to be seen, but because we aren't, we hide. Then, when safe people finally offer us the chance to be seen, we still pull away. Being understood feels both threatening and appealing; it's both the venom and the antidote. I've seen this frequently—in clients, strangers, people I've known, and former versions of myself. It's the constant emotional whiplash of trying to love in a world that keeps handing you grief. So, when the opportunity comes to be fully known, the fear of vulnerability meets us. We question if it's okay to trust it. Therefore, withdrawing has many internal voices:

- "I don't want to be a burden to anyone."
- "People don't really care anyway."
- "Every time I open up, it backfires."
- "If I disappear quietly, no one will even notice."
- "I'll reconnect when I feel better."
- "They wouldn't understand even if I tried to explain."

There's an invisible grief in withdrawing—a grief most people never see because it looks like a choice from the outside. They say, "They've pulled away. They always keep to themselves." But what they don't see is what happens in the space between distance and desire. In every step back, there's the loss of:

- I'm grieving what I want to be,
- I'm grieving what I should be, and
- I'm grieving the way I wish I could show up but can't.

The Releaser Root doesn't come as an authoritarian ruler, dictating what you can and cannot have, when to let go, or how long you're allowed to hold on. Instead, it arrives with empathy, compassion, and a profound understanding of who you are. It leads you toward the freedom of releasing your fear of being seen. No longer will you have to shrink or play small to accommodate others who are uncomfortable with your authenticity. The Releaser Root helps you step into your true self, and be surrounded by people ready to embrace you as you are—and as you are becoming.

It may feel impossible right now—maybe even unthinkable—but there are more people who will love, accept, and celebrate all of you than you've ever been led to believe. Your world may not have shown you that yet, but the world itself is much bigger than you've been taught. If you can release what you've clung to, just long enough to take hold of something new, you might be surprised to discover that your past, your pain, your victories, and your identity can be fully embraced.

You Are the Clock

Release isn't a checklist. It's not something you master or finally get right. It's a conversation between you and what you've carried—an honest, trembling pause where you admit: *I've held this long enough.*

You're not learning how to let go of everything. You're learning how to loosen your grip where you no longer need to hold so tight. Some pieces of you were never meant to be discarded—the wisdom, the strength, the tenderness you fought for. But some things have stayed past their time. And now, you're learning how to make space—for breath, for becoming, for what's next.

Healing isn't linear, and neither is carrying the grief that can't be fixed. You already know that. Some days you move forward. Other days you slip backward. But even in the slipping, there's still movement. Every quiet release, every small moment of self-honesty, counts. It all counts. You don't need to have it all figured out. You don't have to be ready for everything. You just need permission—for this moment—to lay down what's become too heavy. And trust that what's waiting on the other side isn't emptiness, but life.

The Releaser Root will always be with you: In your capacity to love yourself. In your willingness to let yourself be seen, even when you feel exposed. In your quiet bravery to whisper, *this version of me can grow*. You're not rushing. You're not forcing. You're becoming. And when the release comes, freedom will rise right alongside it.

Friendly Recap

- Growth brings grief, and grief brings growth. The two are often inseparable.
- It is okay to grieve what is no longer working.
- As you reflect on your life, what is the largest block that's preventing you from releasing aspects of your Shapeshifter Identity? What's one step that you can take to move toward letting go?

Chapter 8

The Practical Side of Releasing

Before we talk about how to release, my Truth Seeker Root compels me to be honest with you: Not everyone has the same freedom to shed all their old roles and masks. For some, performance isn't only a habit—it's protection. It's tied to financial stability, safety in dangerous environments, and terrible and unjust repercussions.

That's why we never demonize the shapeshifter, because it serves a critical purpose. It got you here, and it might be needed to help keep you here. This doesn't mean release is out of reach. It might mean that you will have to discover ways to have **micro-releases**—small, intentional moments where you allow yourself to step into who you are. It's finding the areas in your life, perhaps compartmentalized, where you can take off the mask with ease.

The world consistently asks you to perform. As the saying goes, "All the world's a stage, and all the men and women merely players."[1] Get curious by saying, "Where in my life can I be me and only me—no scripts and no edits? Do I feel safe being me when I am alone?" This process is not easy. This is a big ask, and yet it is what is required for us to operate in this world, and truly know ourselves, not for who others want us to be, but for who we have always been. In that, whether it's the shapeshifting we *consciously* do to feel protected, or the identity we've integrated, there is power and intimacy—the kind that comes from seeing yourself.

Releasing the Need to Be Constantly Validated

Validation is a slippery slope, and in the beginning, it's hard to find the right balance—if there is one. When we haven't been affirmed for our goodness or seen in our hardship, we wonder: *What's normal? Am I doing it all wrong?* This is common among people who carry histories of childhood trauma, grief, or who fall outside of what society judges as "neurotypical."

As someone who sits with people through life transitions, I receive all sorts of questions: Is it okay to be sad if my parents were physically present but emotionally absent? Can you have trauma if you grew up middle-class? Is it okay if I'm crying over my child, sibling, parent, friend, or partner, years later? Do people with ADHD generally struggle with listening or zoning out, or is it my grief? They seek reassurance that their way of processing the world differently doesn't indicate they are inherently defective, but instead, that their biological wiring, experiences, and environment have shaped how they move through life.

---

[1] William Shakespeare's play *As You Like It*.

Validation helps us find and reset our internal compass. It's also comforting. You go to a grief group, Alcoholics Anonymous, a mental health therapy group, and you hear stories of people who share similar experiences. You realize, "Wow, I'm not the only one. They get it!" You speak to other parents or those who are single and think, "They understand me! What a relief!"

It feels good to be held by someone who knows. For example, I will forever be indebted to my early widow friends, especially those whom I met when I was a twenty-something grieving the death of my soulmate. When I found someone in my age group who could speak the same wounded language as I did, I cried. The parts of me that sat in hardship and pain had found a home to abide in. It was helpful to know there were others who understood my perspective on life at that time and could serve as proof that overwhelming suffering would lessen.

This relief is common. Shame begins to loosen when someone realizes they're not an outlier. One of my first clients sat across from me in tears because every woman she knew seemed to have a great relationship with their mom, and she felt alone in not having that with hers. I expressed that the relationship with my mother started out less than perfect, and she said, "Really? I feel seen. I'm not the weirdo or the one who has all the problems. Maybe there's hope for us, for me."

When you tell your story you allow someone to feel assured in theirs. Not everyone will experience the transformation of healing. But everyone—and I mean *everyone*—will experience losses in their lives. However, telling our stories doesn't make the pain and the internal body sensations leave. How many times have we heard someone retell the same painful story (or maybe that person is us)? Yesterday's pain shows up in the life we're living today.

However, if we aren't using it to consistently fine-tune our intuition, we risk becoming dependent on validation and suffer when it isn't given. The reassurance you're looking for grows when you stop rehearsing other people's opinions and listen to the wisdom you've earned. We don't ask anyone for permission to feel what happens in our own skin. If you have a headache, you don't ask, "Is it okay that this hurts? Am I allowed to be uncomfortable?" You simply acknowledge it. Your emotional cues and intuition deserve the same respect.

Building Internal Validation: The Alignment Exercise

Self-doubt lives in the tension between what we think and what we feel. We may say, "I know I'm allowed to feel this way," but still sense in our bodies it's not safe or acceptable to do so. This mismatch—called incongruence—leaves us looking outward for reassurance, because inside, we don't fully trust what we know or feel.

Realigning our body and mind builds confidence. The more your thoughts, emotions, and physical presence work together, the less you will depend upon others to tell you who you are, and what's permissible for you to feel, think, and choose.

A way to practice honoring your intuition, and thereby validate yourself, is an exercise I use with clients. It seems elementary in the beginning and almost too simple to work. But with practice, those who have used it build self-confidence. As a by-product, the Releaser Root does its work in the background, and the dependency on others fades away.

Amanda and I met because she was struggling to face a recent loss. I noticed that when she spoke, her body language said one thing while her words said another. She'd say she felt happy about something but never smiled or expressed joyful movement. Whenever she said she was doing okay, her body seemed tired and disconnected.

When I gently invited her to talk about her most recent loss, her whole body responded first. She subtly shifted her chair an inch farther from mine. Then she forced a small smile and said, "We can talk about it," while breaking eye contact mid-sentence.

"Before we do," I said to her, "I want to make sure all of you is okay with talking about the loss. Take a moment to see if there's anything inside of you that doesn't want to discuss it."

Amanda paused for a moment and nodded yes. "Yeah, I think it's okay," she said with uncertainty.

I wasn't convinced. While she verbally said yes, her shaky voice and stiff body continued to speak otherwise.

"Does any of this feel scary, or just a bit uncomfortable?" I asked.

"I'm not sure. I really don't want to talk about it. I tend to avoid hard stuff. I'm afraid it'll go too deep and send me into a downward spiral."

"On a scale of zero to ten, with ten being extremely intense, how strong would you say that avoidance feeling is?"

"Hmm . . . somewhere around a seven."

(continued)

(continued)

"What if we honored the part that wants to avoid the conversation? We can say, 'I don't want to talk about this,' and as you're saying it, you can motion that you're pushing me away. I'll do the same in solidarity with you."

Amanda and I began to say, "I don't want to talk about this," and we motioned our hands against each other. I encouraged her to use her full body, motioning her hands and arms outward to her sides, toward the floor, above her, and especially at me. After about thirty seconds or so I asked her, "What's it like to do this?"

"It feels congruent. It's like what I feel and what I'm thinking actually match for once." And you doing it with me made me feel like I wasn't going to be judged for not talking about it." This time she smiled, and her body relaxed.

"On that same scale of zero to ten, how intense does that avoidance feel now?"

"Somewhere around a three. I feel more empowered now."

We didn't speak about the details of Amanda's loss that session. Instead, we focused on honoring her feelings. We did similar exercises for matching her body language to how she felt inside. I encouraged her to do the same throughout the week. After another session or two, I noticed whenever she said she was having a good day, she said so with a smile. When she said she was sad, she let her eyes get teary. When we reached a hard part of the conversation, she paused and said it wasn't something she wanted to talk about right now, but she was open to discussing it later.

Amanda was able to honor her feelings by honoring how they showed up for her in thought and body. When her alignment strengthened, she sought less validation from me, and from our conversations, less reassurance from others. Her mind-body connection provided its own internal wisdom she could hear.

When I lead groups, I'll often pair two people together and have them practice mind-body congruency exercises, one person speaks, and the other mirrors their body language. Noticing the alignment, or lack thereof, between what's said and expressed helps us see ourselves better while sharpening our discernment toward others.

The Releaser Root helps us cultivate a unified identity. When your mind-body connection becomes consistent, you experience yourself as someone who is safe, stable, and confident, and others experience you this way too. This is how character steadiness is built. It allows you to respond according to who you are and live from that place instead of getting frustrated by the moments when you act one way yet feel another.

Now, this isn't to be confused with reacting from our feelings. *Emotions are a great servant, but a poor master.* If someone at work makes an insulting remark, your feelings of anger want you to yell back, even if you know it's best not to. You can honor the anger by realizing a boundary of yours has been crossed—they were disrespectful—and respond by speaking up for yourself, reporting it to human resources, or taking another supportive action. In this way, your mind and body are still aligned. You felt the feeling, understood its message, and made a wise decision for how to respond.

Teaching Note: A Look Behind the Scenes

At first glance, it might seem contradictory: If we're trying to lessen avoidance, wouldn't encouraging Amanda to lean into it make things worse? The relief she experienced from honoring her avoidance could feel rewarding and suggest she should keep doing it. But avoidance isn't the problem—not feeling safe is.

In Amanda's case, she feared that talking about her loss would make her spiral downward. That's a reasonable fear. While I didn't need to ask her this directly for the work we were doing, her comment—"You doing it with me made me feel like I wasn't going to be judged"—revealed what was happening underneath: She was afraid and our work together cocreated safety. When she felt safe, her system could tolerate more emotion, and her pull toward avoidance naturally softened.

Now You Try

Note: While this work, like all exercises in this chapter, supports self-awareness, some individuals may benefit from working alongside an identity and grief specialist, such as myself, or a trauma-trained therapist to safely explore deeper layers.

Step One: Name It

Choose one thought or emotion—something *small* that *feels safe* to explore right now (don't re-traumatize yourself by choosing something too big). Say it aloud or write it down.

Step Two: Notice It

Ask yourself, "How does my body feel as I notice this emotion or thought?" You can either make a mental note of this or write it down. I encourage writing it down because it externalizes what you feel. This helps you to place separation between your thoughts and emotions.

Step Three: Express It

Let your body express small, safe gestures. If you feel like pulling away, do so. If you feel sad, perhaps give yourself permission to cry or speak your feelings into a journal or voice note. If your body requires movement, perhaps take a short walk or do a stretch or two. These small physical cues help your mind and body speak the same language without forcing or escalating the emotion.

Daily Practice

You can continue practicing alignment throughout your day. You may want to start alone or in safe environments with *safe* people. As we discussed earlier, there may be times when it doesn't feel wise to fully express what you're feeling. When it's appropriate, allow the Releaser Root to guide you into small micro-releases—letting your mind and body gently come into alignment.

Releasing the "Healed Enough" Mask

Traditionally, only those who were in the healing fields and seeking therapy were privy to therapeutic language. Under these conditions, therapy-speak was backed by evidence-based research and used correctly. However, at the start of the pandemic in 2020, mental health took a huge turn. While many were in lockdown at home or practicing social distancing, therapists and healers took to the internet, podcasts, traditional media, and other platforms to explain the feelings many were experiencing.

This was great, it helped make mental health *knowledge* more accessible and offered understanding. For the first time on a national scale (and in some ways, global), mental health had entered mainstream culture. This led to an uptick in coaches, business professionals, and those with large online audiences using therapy-speak, which was new for society at large and proved beneficial.

However, as with many cause-and-effect cycles, the pendulum swung. The more information that was put out, the more people started using it—but without the proper context, nuance, or *applied* understanding. We began seeing an increase in people talking about others "being toxic," which thereby led many to "focus on their healing," and "stay to themselves," until they were "healed enough."

On the other side of the spectrum, a different group emerged—people claiming to be fully healed, so much so that they began calling out those who weren't. Ironically, this is one of the clearest signs that more healing is still needed. Healers build people up; they don't use shame, rejection, or superiority. In fact, they often speak about their own shortcomings—not *for* validation, pity, or attention, but *from* transparency and vulnerability, because they genuinely want peace and healing for others.

While much of this language was meant to help, *knowledge acquisition without knowledge application doesn't lead to transformation.* What we see now is a culture that acknowledges the dragon in the dungeon but hasn't released it. Therefore, we face each other—and ourselves—wounded. Without the Releaser Root at work, claiming the true treasure of healing and identity is impossible.

Earlier in this book, we learned that the Shapeshifter Root tries to disguise itself as the Releaser Root. It wears the mask of Performative Healing. Sometimes it looks like the person who says, "I'm over that" or "I've grown beyond that," while continuously returning to the same stories, the same wounds, and the same angles.

When we've healed from bad relationships, we don't dwell on who hurt us. When we've healed our parental wounds, we don't loop around to what our mother and father didn't do. When our discernment improves and our relationships strengthen, we stop centering the people we've deemed toxic and dysfunctional. When you change, the conversation changes with you.

How to Lean into Healing

1. **Name the fear behind the mask:**
   - What do I fear will happen if people know I'm still struggling?
   - Where am I still confusing healing with the need to protect an image?
   - Am I afraid that being in need might mean I need others?
2. **Acknowledge the first half of the trauma bargain we've made such as:**
   - If they see this part of me, they'll reject me.
   - If they see this unhealed part of me, I'll lose credibility.
   - If they see this unhealed part of me, I'll feel humiliated.
3. **Practice safe transparency in small, controlled spaces such as:**
   - I'm still learning how to deal with this.
   - I'm still processing it, and I'll get back to you once I do.
   - I'm struggling with . . .
4. **Separate your worth from your progress. Everyone has wounds.**
   - Healing is not a public performance or what we do for approval.
   - Everyone is either healing, taking a break from healing, or needing it.

Not every area of your life is wounded. You have healed areas already.

The Releaser Root reminds you that you don't have to tell yourself, "I need to arrive." We are always arriving. As writer and philosopher Aldous Huxley said, "Every ceiling, when reached, becomes a floor."

A Moment of Pause

Inhale deeply, then exhale. Repeat this twice more. Now see if you can sense your heartbeat. Can you hear it? Feel it? Can you find anything in your environment that makes you feel safe? It might be a closed door, an open one, the quiet of being alone, or the presence of being with someone you trust. Safety could mean that right now, at this moment, the greatest privacy you have is the sole access to your thoughts. Whatever it is, it helps to take a moment to pause—including when you're reading. Remember identity work isn't always easy. It makes us think, feel, and reflect. Mix in all the other things you have experienced and might be carrying, and it can feel like a lot. Let this be your moment to pause. One last time: As you inhale, imagine warmth and comfort flowing into your body. Then exhale stress, whatever feels heavy or unnecessary. Let it leave you. Imagine it flowing out on your exhales. Inhale, exhale. Inhale, exhale.

My Truth Versus Reality

Before we can release anything, we have to understand what we're holding. The Releaser Root isn't just about letting go of pain; it's about letting go of the interpretations pain turned into identity. Most of us didn't adopt beliefs like "I'm unlovable," "I'm too much," or "I'm not chosen" on purpose—those identities were shaped by how we made sense of what happened. When our nervous system was overwhelmed, what we felt became what we believed, and what we believed became who we thought we were.

Releasing means loosening the grip of those interpretations so your identity can be restored. This is where the difference between *my* truth and *the* truth becomes essential. This is not gaslighting—which denies your reality; this invites you to explore the meaning you attached to it.

The trauma we experience alters our internal sight. Reality gets filtered through how it felt to us. That's why siblings raised in the same house can walk away from the same moment with completely different experiences. They may even remember the facts differently.

It's not just about what happened or why. It's about to whom it happened, and how that person's inner world made sense of it. After a long day of work, one child might perceive their parent's aloofness as "Dad doesn't love me."

Another child might think, "Dad is tired." Based upon their interpretation, the child will either have more external understanding or internalized self-judgment. The perception trap often confuses our truths with reality.

The trap looks like: "People stopped checking in on me after my loss because they didn't care."

The reality might be: "They haven't developed the capacity to sit with someone grieving or might be suffering internal pain themselves."

The trap tells us: "People don't like talking to me."

The reality might be: "I need to become a better listener by not interrupting people."

The Releaser Root helps you recognize that your identity was never the story your pain told about you. You're allowed to set down the interpretation that made you small, frightened, or unworthy. You're allowed to see yourself with new eyes. Releasing is the moment you say, "That was part of my story, but it isn't the whole truth of who I am."

How to Break Free of Harmful "Truths"

Dr. Brené Brown, a researcher and author, encourages people to say, *The story I am telling myself is. . .*[2] Doing this challenges our perceptions by positioning it as a story, rather than a fact.

For example:

The story I'm telling myself is . . .

- ". . .I cry too much or none at all; therefore, I'm not grieving right."
- ". . .if it wasn't physical abuse, then it wasn't traumatic."
- ". . .if I stop being the go-to person in my family, no one will know how to survive."

---

[2] Brené Brown, "Brené Brown on How to Reckon with Emotion and Change Your Narrative," O, The Oprah Magazine, September 2015.

We can also see how we tell ourselves stories about others. *The story I'm telling myself about them is . . .*

- "They correct me because they don't think I'm smart."
  Reality: Many people correct us out of love, because they want to increase the knowledge we already have.
- "They're being kind because they pity me, not because they care."
  Reality: People do care for you and are saddened to hear you're hurting.
- "They're just waiting for me to mess up so they can leave."
  Reality: They might not notice or be bothered by the small things I think will push them away. My fear is telling the story, not their actions.
- "They're calm because they don't care."
  Reality: Some people process inwardly.

But wait. Can two things be true at the same time? Yes. Your parent may have been emotionally unavailable, tired, or unequipped to meet your pain. And you may have walked away from that experience feeling deeply unloved and unwanted. Both can be true. That's the power of complexity. But sometimes, "both/and" becomes a trap. It keeps us endlessly explaining harm, walking in mental circles, and distorting our present-day reality.

For example:

- *Yes, relocating gave me new opportunities, and yes, I still keep rehearsing the loss of belonging instead of building a new community.*
- *Yes, I've gained wisdom with age, and yes, I can grieve the loss of my prime—but if I keep circling that tension, I never step into who I am now.*

The Releaser Root reminds us that healing doesn't always live in the nuance—it sometimes lives in the decision. When I was a kid, the comic books I read let you choose the story's ending. If you wanted the main character to have one fate—you started reading the ending from a different page. If you wanted the main character to have another fate, you continued. Your life gets to be the same. One decision keeps you tethered to the past. Another lets you walk forward.

What Micro-Releasing Truths Looks Like

- **Either** I name what happened to me **and** learn how it shaped me—**or** I keep living like I'm the problem, instead of someone who experienced a problem.
- **Either** my parent(s) lacked capacity, **and** I release the belief that this made me unworthy of love—**or** I continue carrying the story that I am not someone others choose, nurture, or stay for.
- **Either** my family struggled financially, **and** I release the belief that I am destined to live in lack—**or** I continue carrying the story that stability, ease, and overflow are things meant for other people, not me.
- **Either** the relationship ended because we were no longer aligned **and** I release the belief that I failed at connection—**or** I continue carrying the story that I am too much, too broken, or too complicated to be chosen again.
- **Either** I was praised only when I performed, **and** I release the belief that I must be flawless—**or** I continue carrying the story that any mistake confirms I'm not enough.
- **Either** I accept that my brain works differently, **and** I learn new ways to break things down so I can follow through—**or** I keep telling myself I'm broken every time I struggle to start.
- **Either** I learn that rest is a part of healing, not a reward for being useful, **and** I release the belief that I must earn my right to slow down—**or** I keep hustling for worth and calling it ambition.

Apply It

Tip: You don't have to do all three steps at once. Try one and check in on how your mind and body feel before *safely* moving on to the next one.

1. Ask yourself what stories you are telling yourself. Begin with, "The story I am telling myself is. . ."
2. Next, ask yourself, what stories you're telling yourself about others. Begin with, "The story I am telling about them is. . ."
3. Lastly, choose your **either/and/or** statement: Either [situation], and I release [action/belief]—or I continue the [story/outcome].

Gentle Note

Releasing what you've held onto can be hard. If you have a trusted person you can do this exercise alongside, it could lighten how the release feels. Often, our identities heal best in relationships (I'll share more on this later). It doesn't have to be complicated—sometimes it's just saying, "I was reading this part of a book about the stories we tell ourselves, and it made me stop and wonder about my own. Here's one example. . ."

If you have a therapist or grief and identity specialist you're working with, you can say, "I read something recently that helped me name a few old beliefs I might have. I think I want to talk through a few of them with you." Or you can write them down and reflect on them in a private journal.

Our Open Wounds Bleed on Others

Sometimes, the stories we tell ourselves began in real harm. We were true victims—something happened to us that we had no power to prevent. In *The Phantom of the Opera*, a play and movie produced by Andrew Lloyd Webber (though it was first a book by Gaston Leroux), the Phantom is introduced as a mysterious menace haunting the Paris Opera House. As the story unfolds, we learn he was once a child with, what was considered in the early 1900s, "a facial deformity." Because of this, the Phantom was abused, mocked, and hidden from the world. As he grows into adulthood, he becomes a talented musician, but also a man consumed by pain.

In the play, a character says to the Phantom, "Haven't you any compassion?"

The Phantom, burning with rage, shouts back, "Compassion? The world had no compassion for me!"

This moment holds a chilling truth: The wounded boy grows up to become the adult villain in someone's story. Unprocessed pain doesn't go away. When we don't release the weight of what happened—when we stay fused with our wound—we risk justifying the harm we cause. *I was hurt, so I hurt others. This isn't selfishness, it's self-preservation.* Sometimes we don't even realize we're bleeding onto others until they quietly walk away.

When we don't heal our wounds, we end up passing on that unhealed pain. What begins as a small fracture—a betrayal, a neglect, a loss—can spread into other parts of our lives and relationships if it's never addressed. Think of it like a cracked tooth: If it's left unattended, bacteria can enter the bloodstream. Similarly, emotional fractures can spread pain in places we never intended. Releasing the suffering that shaped us benefits everyone. It impacts us and the people we care for, love, and desire a healthy relationship with. It also clears space for an identity that isn't built from the wound, but from who you are beyond it.

And here's the good news: while infection spreads, so does healing. What the Phantom never realized is that if he had tended to his pain—if someone had helped him see he deserved to receive compassion—he might have found the capacity to give it, even when it hadn't been given to him. And that's the hope for us, too.

When Unspoken Needs Breed Identity Distortion

Back in the Shapeshifter Root, we explored how many of us expect others to read our needs—especially when we've spent a lifetime reading theirs. For some, life taught you asking for what you need leads to disappointment, criticism, or abandonment. Therefore, you stay quiet to please others and keep the peace. But here's the thing: *peacekeeping isn't the same as peacemaking*. In relationships, compliance looks like:

- Going along with decisions you don't agree with.
- Smiling through discomfort.
- Saying "I'm fine" when you're not.

Over time, resentment builds until it explodes. The blow-up wasn't the result of one small issue. It was the product of unmet needs, ignored feelings, and fractures that never had the chance to heal. Often, the people around us were unaware of the problems. You convinced them that the mask you wore was you, and they believed it. They didn't understand the unspoken pressure building. When it finally cracked, it felt like a storm leaving behind relational damage that could require years of repair. Much of this catastrophe could have been mitigated with honest communication. Sometimes, it's not that people don't care—it's that they don't know how to meet needs we've never expressed.

Silent harm looks like:

- Refusing help when it's offered, then resenting people for "never being there."
- Pretending everything's fine to avoid conflict and then erupting in anger when we've reached our limit.
- Assuming malice where there may only be misunderstanding, then withdrawing without clarifying.
- Creating exit strategies (emotional detachment, withholding affection) in lieu of voicing what's hurting us.

This isn't about blame. It's about the truth of your needs and emotions. Releasing pain means letting go of requiring people to guess what you need. *Silent resentment doesn't protect you—it corrodes the foundation of your relationships.* Communication is vulnerable, but silence isn't the safe option; it's a time bomb. The longer you hold it in, the more explosive *and* damaging the release is.

The Release Isn't a Single Moment

How lovely would it be to simply release the habits, mindsets, and feelings we no longer want? But after spending years—even a lifetime—building one way of life, it's natural to feel the pull to return to it. We fall into old patterns, sometimes getting burned again, then dust ourselves off to try better next time.

Making mistakes is a sign that we are living. Having ups and downs is what makes you human. You don't have to get it right the first time, or the second and third. You'll have moments when you realize, "Oh! I said I was over this, and I would move differently when this happened," only after it's too late to make changes. This is a part of the process. We make micro-releases as we go along, and little by little, the small portions add up. You'll wake up one day and realize that how you handled a situation was different than before; you'll be shocked by it, questioning if it was right, yet hopefully, proud.

But know that progress comes with challenges. It will be harder to release what is still serving you in some way—even if you know in the long run it's unsupportive or forces you to shapeshift. Survival is important, and we do what we must to get through, provide for ourselves the best we can, and maintain what portions we have. Knowing how to survive is as much a gift as it is a talent. We don't shun ourselves for it. We don't criticize why we've taken on these skills and the myriad reasons we feel forced to hold onto them. And when times are tough, we want to stick to what we know. It doesn't make you a bad person. It makes you human.

The fact that you are recognizing these patterns is progress and the first step to making any change. We evolve over time. What serves you today might not serve you years from now. You might decide to make micro-releases in the future. The beautiful aspect of life is that you get to determine who you want to be, and more importantly, who you know yourself as.

This is the gift of the Releaser Root. It gives you the power of choice in ways you may not have had before. It allows you to release the pain that is no longer yours to hold and put down the burdens you inherited. As a root that offers freedom, it's here to support you as your life unfolds and your grief is carried. Most of all, it encourages new sprouts to grow from above and deeply roots itself as new layers begin to build.

Friendly Recap

- Releasing doesn't mean pretending the past never happened. It means refusing to let old wounds set the terms of your future.
- Release isn't a single goodbye: it's choosing, again and again, not to live under yesterday's rules.
- The Releaser Root isn't about discarding your story; it's making room for a new one. What part of your story would you like to build newness around?

Root Four

THE BUILDER

The More the Merrier (Sometimes)

I was ready to go! My music teacher told the class we had a huge project to do, and I just knew I was going to do well. I had been playing piano since I was five, and I wasn't worried. I was already planning how to ace it. That is, until she said the words I hated most: "This is a group project."

Oh, nah. A group project? C'mon. This isn't even an orchestra or a piano duet. Why a group? I hated group projects. It wasn't that I didn't like working with people. I was a friendly kid who got along with nearly everybody. What I didn't like was when we mixed people and projects together because somehow, when the groups were assigned, I always got screwed over with the pickings.

All right, let's be hopeful, I thought. *Maybe I'll get lucky.* Yeah, okay. The teacher was already assigning groups and, of course, I was paired with the "I don't have it, but what happened was. . ." kid, or the one who went dumpster diving in her backpack, taking papers out, loudly shuffling others' stuff around, forever "looking" for the homework she said she had done.

The teacher told us to get into our groups and talk about how we wanted to divide and conquer the project. "Consider it a head start class." I mumbled under my breath, *a real head start would've been letting me do it alone.* I turned my chair to face the other two kids, and as I had expected, they wanted to talk about everything other than the project. Now, I wasn't a goody-two-shoes or a student who had to be the overachiever. But I'd be damned if I failed something this easy given how much music I already had within me. Eventually, the teacher came by and got us together; everyone had their assignments and knew what their responsibilities were.

A week went by, and I had all my stuff together. I told my classmates if they needed help, I had their back. From sheet music to simple melodies, I had brought in metronomes and music history books and CDs—I had it all covered. I didn't care if they used my resources, but I wanted a good grade. When I checked on what they needed, they said they hadn't started but they were good. We were gonna be fine. *The lies.*

Two days before the presentation was due, I was the only one who had done the work. I was annoyed. I had realized that I would likely have to go above and beyond, making my part extra stellar if theirs fell through, so at least I could carry my part well. It was a good thing I did. The day the project was due, when the other groups presented, some people had their stuff and some didn't. But my group? We were totally unprepared.

The teacher called on us, and I grabbed my trifold boards and music. The other two students just stared at me stupidly. "We didn't do the work," one mouthed. "Give us some of your note cards."

The teacher told us, "I'll give you all a few more days, but I'm dropping you down a letter grade."

Now, I know I could have pretended they did the work. I could've been "a team player" and filled them in. Did it matter who got the credit? We could all win, right? But that wasn't the point. I was fed up with building *for* people instead of *with* them. I was tired of having others applaud me for doing well, then wanting a piece of the pie they weren't willing to contribute to.

I protested. "I'll present solo." I set up my stuff in the front of the class and before the teacher could tell me no, she said, "Well...I guess you can present alone if you like, Ashley, and the others can bring theirs next week."

I remember being so happy when I finished that school year. No more trios! What I didn't know was that all of life is a group project. You can be prepared and gifted, yet still encounter people who bring nothing to the table. Expanding our capacity helps us deal with these people when going solo isn't an option. Growth shows us how to build better relationships when we're given the chance or, in the least, to be okay going solo until we find our tribe.

The Builder Root

This fourth root gives you the blueprint for rebuilding your identity when the people you counted on drop the ball, disappeared, or expected you to carry it all. It's about what happens after the loss.

The Builder Root asks: Who are you becoming now that everything has changed—especially when the people around you haven't? When change uproots your world, most people talk about survival—*I'm taking it one day at a time.* While that isn't a bad thing, it helps to know which tools you should be using. If you build it right the first time, you can prevent it from crumbling later.

This root is about construction, the slow, intentional, and often lonely act of identity rebuilding. Here's the part no one tells you: Building isn't always fun and exciting. Like going to work every day, you have to do what you don't want to do so you can get to the things you do want to do. Real building work is daily—in the way you rest and take action—and much of it is relational. You have to decide:

- Who should you build alongside?
- What tools are serving you, and which are broken coping mechanisms?
- How do you build the person you'll live with every day—you?

Building your new identity is interwoven with the connections you make because that's when who we are gets tested and proven. It's easy to feel confident when we're alone. But the moment someone doubts us or names us as something we aren't, that confidence can collapse. Many of us have lived this—steady in session or at home, only to crumble in a group or family conversation. If that's you, there's no shame. The goal isn't to never falter; it's to notice when it happens and ask, "What's keeping me from being grounded in who I am?" Dismantling that obstacle is where the real work is.

Building Isn't Starting Over

Loss—whether through death, disconnection, or transition—can leave you feeling like you're starting from scratch. Like life yanked the blueprint out of your hands and said, "Try again. This time, with less." And yes, some of us have lost *everything*. Starting again feels insulting. Impossible. Cruel. So let me be clear: I'm not here to minimize your grief or sprinkle glitter over the ashes. I *am* here to remind you: You're not starting over from *there*. You're starting again from *here*, and that's not the same thing. You're not building from the version of you that didn't know loss. You're building from the version that has scars that offer wisdom, discernment, and fortitude. That's your foundation now.

It's not a restart. It's a reset—like a diamond being moved from one jewelry setting into another. Your core is unchanged, still gleaming and forged by the fire of every trial you've faced, and infinitely more precious than you often allow yourself to believe. However, the setting that once cradled you may have fractured: its edges dulled, its walls worn thin, unable to honor the brilliance you carry. A reset isn't about diminishing your worth; it's about choosing a new cradle—one that is worthy of you and reflects each facet of your resilience as you enter into a new light.

Chapter 9

Hope-PTSD

Society speaks of healing as if it's a return. But some losses don't come back. The child is still gone. The soulmate is not coming home. The loved one is not reawakening. The years loss swallowed doesn't reverse the clock when you've recognized what it's stolen. The diagnosis remains, the financial account, once full of investments, is empty. We look in the mirror, and we are older than we were yesterday, and the day before that, and the time before everything first shattered before our eyes.

We wonder, *what's the point?* If there are certain aspects of life that cannot be restored, what does healing mean for the ones who survive? Healing can feel like a cruel suggestion; you're being asked to build a new life with pieces you didn't choose, and there are pieces you won't get back. We have scars, and some of the wounds we carry are still bleeding.

Healing is for the incomplete.
It's for those whose stories are half-told, wrongly written, misguided, and torn beyond recognition.

Healing is for those to whom it has been
explicitly said or implied
that you are not enough or too much or never right
for anything or anyone or anyplace.
Healing is for those who are tired, and weary,
and confused—left alone, unseen, and forgotten.
It's for those whose mouths cannot fathom speaking
the silent cries they weep at night or the terrors
they encounter by day.

Myths have taught us that we reach for healing to recover, restore, and rediscover. We are told it is for the lucky ones, the people who believe in the miraculous and supernatural. Healing is none of this. It is for the least likely—the ones who fall without anyone to help them get up, the ones who say, "That's not for me because. . ." and "I'm always overlooked." We don't reach for healing because we've gotten it right or because we are right. We reach for healing because it gives us hope, the most courageous thing we carry in a suffering world.

When Wanting Something Scares You

Hope is like throwing a penny into a wishing well. You stand there, professing the thing you want, and here comes life picking your pockets. It's bad enough you believe that tossing money into a gum-filled pool will be helpful, but now, life is taking what's left. The Builder Root comes in to teach you that true hope isn't about guarantees; it's about daring to invest in possibility, even when you know you might get robbed.

Still, after being burned so many times, the slightest act of hope can be met with hesitation. You start asking yourself: What do I stand to lose this time? The answer may be "a whole lot," or "not much," or "I can't afford another setback," depending upon the situation. That makes sense. Hope is strong, but it's also fragile. Most businesses fail, divorce rates are high, death happens without notice, and life sends curveballs.

I realized this in my early twenties. Naively, I thought I had life mapped out, and, darling, I was wrong. People said "You're young, you're strong, you have a bright future ahead of you." I thought I was invincible (as many young people do). I had a wonderful man, Jason, whom I loved and respected, and he cherished and loved me in return. We had clear goals and plans for what we wanted together. When I looked at life, I saw a full box of crayons—they were sharp, fresh, and all the colors were in place. Then life came back and laughed at me. Like a bully, it broke my crayons, ripped up my plans, and shoved me into the mud.

Maybe you've been there too. Life wasn't perfect, but you were managing. You had a plan that felt known and certain. You were finally getting it together or were almost there. Your relationship was decent. The kids were happy. The family finally acted like they loved each other, or you accepted they wouldn't. You mustered up the courage to leave the relationships that weren't working and get your health under control. Or maybe you told yourself, "I have time" because life set you up to believe that.

I get it. One day I was happy, and the next day, I was Jason's widow and then Michael's the second time around. It seemed crazy that as we were planning and enjoying life, death was around the corner. That's why I don't blame anyone for feeling how they do toward walking in their True Identity. It seems risky.

In researching hope, I spent a month, daily, interviewing adults who had experienced a form of hardship, change, or loss. While a few were optimistic and excited to have hope (we'll talk about this shortly), many were skeptical. "It's hard to believe in the good when bad events keep occurring," many told me. It was so prevalent, I coined a term for it—**Hope-PTSD**. When you've been burned so many times by promises, opportunities, or people, the tiniest spark of possibility feels threatening. It's bracing for the worst at your own celebration because trusting for something good to happen feels riskier than expecting a bad outcome.

Society labels it as "giving up" on ourselves, our dreams, on living a life. What they don't know is *not* hoping is a nervous system strategy for some people. When your body mislabels growth as dangerous, removing hope becomes the logical defense to avoid disappointment and potentially "wasted" energy. Therefore, dismissing hope isn't lazy—it's self-preservation. Learning when the strategy has expired, and how to prevent it from keeping you from an unfulfilled life, is challenging.

It's important to note while Hope-PTSD is a term I coined to express what we feel, it is neither clinical nor medical in nature. It suggests a series of patterns after loss and tragedy people might experience. For example, in the qualitative interviews I conducted, Hope-PTSD appeared as:

- Being on high alert whenever something positive shows up.
- Avoiding most to all celebrations. *"Don't get too excited, it'll blow up in your face."*
- The struggle or inability to plan for the future, i.e. create a six-month, one-year, or five-year plan.
- Having reluctance toward believing in the possibility of good *specifically* because of lived patterns of unfavorable past experiences.
- Fear of slowing down when life is good because you fear the next bad moment is around the corner.

How does this impact your True Identity? Hope-PTSD can cause us to become unmotivated in pursuing our goals, withdraw from *good* people to prevent pain that we *imagine* might happen, and stop engaging in new opportunities—including those that are safe and make us feel well-supported. Have you ever wondered what the catch was when life handed you a genuine, no-strings-attached win? You struggle to trust the *good* thing because you're expecting the *bad* one to show up.

For those who have spent a significant portion of their lives in survival mode, positive expectations don't fit into the equation. As one interviewee in my research said, "There's no hope in survival. It's either you survive or you don't."

Disappointment after disappointment, missed opportunity after missed opportunity, hardship after hardship, life has convinced you that good things don't last. You fight to get through to the next moment. And sometimes, all it takes is one terrible event to lead you to believe this: Your health or finances decline shortly before or after you've retired. The possibility of having children crumbles because of infertility. You feel disheartened after the engagement breaks off. *I didn't anticipate being single, or without kids, or in this circumstance at this age.* When you look to the future, you don't see the one you envisioned.

It's why having community (which we'll talk about in Chapter 11) is helpful. Often, hope is too heavy to carry alone. Sometimes it's a friend, a group, an adolescent, or taking up volunteer work that holds hope for you until you can pick it up again. You don't have to hold onto hope alone.

Hope for a Lost Identity

Rachel was a smart woman who had a great sense of humor, a likeable personality, and a heart that kept expanding.

She loved children and wanted to become a teacher. But after some unfortunate situations—the betrayal of a romantic partner, her grandfather's death, and insurmountable debt, she gave up on her goals. I remember her saying, "Maybe that's a sign that I wasn't meant to do this. The universe is pushing me in a different direction."

"A sign? Rachel, this isn't a movie," I said to her. "Nobody is sending prophetic signals to discourage you after a tragedy. If life were giving out signs, I'd get them too, saying, 'Ashley, don't eat the second bowl of ice cream.'"

Her good humor kicked in and she laughed, "I know. When I'm not stuck in my feelings, I tell myself that. Right now, I'm angry but I'll get over it. I'm okay with never getting married or doing anything with kids."

My heart ached for her; I had seen this too many times. Have you ever noticed how we do that? We talk about how we don't care and "it is what it is" and that we're not thinking about whatever we were hoping for. Yet, we're watching movies about it, reading books on it, scrolling through social media, or getting triggered every time someone in our lives shows up with what we wanted. We get good at masking our desires and dismissing what we need, and all for the sake of preventing a wounded heart.

When I think of you, friend, I only wonder what dreams you've convinced yourself you no longer want to avoid a possible letdown. Rachel said she didn't care about relationships, but if she saw a proposal video, a wedding dress, or was invited to be a bridesmaid, she showed up to my office saying she was jealous or incredibly sad. The manifestation of hope in other's lives is painful when it contrasts against the devastation in ours.

And that's the thing about hope. It slips into the envy we won't admit, plays in the songs we skip too fast, the videos we grow angry over online. Hope peeks from behind ego's door, watching and waiting for us to get tired of pretending we don't want more than the life we're living. It asks us to believe in it. The Builder Root encourages you to choose a life stitched with courage and threaded with grief and wanting.

To be hopeful is to be vulnerable, and the only way to fully live out who you are.

For many, that's terrifying. The more we admit to wanting something, the more we open ourselves up to the risk of not getting it. But here's what I've learned: Hope isn't about certainty. It's not about knowing something good will happen.

Hope is about allowing yourself to believe that
something good *could* happen.
It's about giving yourself another option,
because sticking with the devil you know
still keeps you in hell.
Hope ushers you out of the flames.

How to *Re*consider Hope

It's not that we're afraid to dream. It's that we've been punished for it before. So here's something for you to try. What's one thing you secretly want, but struggle to admit to yourself? If your mind goes blank or instantly pushes the question away, there's usually something standing guard. Something that says, "It's not safe to want that. Don't go there."

When hope has felt too costly to keep, it becomes easier to block it than risk the pain again.

That *something* is what I call a **hope barrier**—the emotional shield we build after we've been disappointed, let down, or betrayed.

Sometimes it shows up as **fear:** *If I hope and it doesn't happen, I'll fall apart.*

Other times, **guilt:** *If I move forward, am I leaving others behind?*

Or even **exhaustion:** *I don't have the energy to think about the future. I'm trying to survive today.*

We block the treasure of a hopeful identity with the wounded dragon guarding it. That dragon is trying to protect us, but it also keeps us from anything new or life-giving. That's why we start with what's manageable, not forced optimism. You don't have to leap into believing again—you only need to make a little room for curiosity.

This is where The LIGHT Method helps. Anxiety often hijacks imagination, pushing us toward worst-case scenarios. LIGHT gives that same imagination a different assignment: to explore what might be possible, gently and without pressure. It's a practical framework for the fragile, in-between moments when you're not ready for big dreams but still want to leave a crack open for change.

LIGHT Method

L—Locate (in the body)
Begin with sensation before story. Notice what shifts in your body when you imagine a desire: a flutter in your chest, heaviness in your stomach, restless legs, warmth in your hands. Even numbness is a response. Naming what your body feels gives you a starting point for hope.

I—Invite
Instead of brushing it off, pause and ask, "Why does this matter to me? What would it look like to let this feeling linger rather than push it away?"

G—Guide
Gently turn your attention toward possibility. Anxiety will want to script worst-case scenarios. Instead, ask, "If things could be even 1% different, what would that look like?" This shifts the imagination from fear toward curiosity.

H—Hold
Hold space for the reaction without needing to solve it. Sit with the question, "Could this be different?" You don't need an immediate answer. Sometimes hope grows simply by being allowed to exist.

T—Tend
Tend to the sprout through one small embodied act: journaling, moving your body, speaking aloud, or sharing with a trusted friend. External action signals to your nervous system that hope is safe enough to nurture.

Whether you've given up on hope, are eager to have it back, or find yourself somewhere in between, I get it. Hope hasn't always aligned with the outcomes you've envisioned. But maybe, when the time is right, you'll reconsider letting it in again. I'm not asking you to put all your eggs in one basket, but perhaps you could crack one open and see what happens. After all, if life is going to surprise you, let it be a good one.

Having Active Hope

Once you've "graduated" to having active hope, you're left trying to make use of it. You think, "I'm ready to evolve into the next version of me, but where do I go from here?" That's when the real work begins because belief alone won't carry you. *Passive hope waits whereas active hope moves.* Active hope isn't hustle or delusion. It's partnership with vision—you're no longer romanticizing the outcome; you're *in relationship* with the *process* of meeting it halfway.

> Active hope makes you a participant of
> who you are, not a spectator.
> Active hope keeps its hands in the dirt—planting, pruning,
> coaxing life, while passive hope leans on the fence,
> longing for what blooms next door.
> Passive hope waits for conditions to change.
> Active hope initiates movement, knowing the journey
> shapes you as much as the outcome.

Passive Hope Versus Active Hope

Passive Hope	**Active Hope**
Delays until all is perfect	Takes a step with uncertainty
Feels like wishing	Feels like building
Avoids risk	Accepts risk
Asks, "What if it goes wrong?"	Asks, "What if it works?"
Romanticizes healing	Reclaims agency

How to Practice Active Hope

You don't need to "figure out" your entire future. Life's too unpredictable for that. We limit our future to what we can see today—not what we're capable of when we're wiser and better years later. For now, pick one longing of yours and become an actionable caretaker of it. This looks like asking yourself:

1. What would it look like to work toward this desire, even if it isn't realized?
2. What's one small thing I can do to support myself in the process?
3. What skills (emotional, relational, spiritual) do I need to live this out?

And "skills" does not mean you need to get a degree, train, or read 100 books on the subject—though it might help. Skills may include:

- Learning to say no
- Improving how you communicate
- Understanding how to prioritize your time
- Being comfortable talking to people
- Practicing resilience in the face of rejection or disappointment

These are skills because just as you learned how to wear a mask, you can learn how to be confident without one. The distance between who you are now and your True Identity isn't fixed.

You build a bridge by acknowledging **three core aspects of yourself:**

1. The beliefs you hold about yourself—which *you're allowed to change*
2. The stories of others you've internalized—which *you get to reject*
3. The skills you need to move through life differently—which *you can build, one at a time*

Ask yourself: "Where have I been waiting too long, wishing, or doubting parts of my life?" You start by taking small steps, which may include:

- Signing up for something before you fully feel "ready"
- Saying yes to what's on your True Identity path, not what will detour you
- Receiving guidance from someone who is successful in that area

Before I entered grief and identity work, I coached writers. Whenever someone said to me, "I want to write a book, but I don't have the time," I'd tell them there are 365 days in a year. If you write one page per day, you'd have enough pages for a book, and most books aren't 365 pages. That means you're allowed to take days off, go slower, and work at a flexible pace. Many of the other choices we make in life are the same—they are all steps, done one day at a time.

We take these steps to release what holds us back. Each choice becomes evidence that you trust yourself enough to let go of the old.

You don't have to wait for the perfect day to return. Your True Identity is still here, patiently waiting for you to step into it.

Hope and fear require belief, but each requires you to trust in a different future.

Choosing You

If you're like most, you don't fear wearing a mask. You fear visibility. But it's not exclusive to others seeing you; it's the fear of *you seeing you.* Taking ownership of the life you have requires you to know yourself. This is hard because you can't unsee what you've seen.

You can't unsee the longings you've buried. You can't deny the ache that's been ignored. You can't pretend the role you've mastered isn't a mask. We experience soul-level intimacy when we make eye contact with who we are.

We speak of being chosen, but the most rewarding choice you'll make is choosing yourself—in full vulnerability, without excuse and performance. On the podcast *The Diary of a CEO,*

Steven Bartlett interviews Alex Hormozi, a serial entrepreneur and philanthropist, who scaled and exited companies, one amassing $46.2 million dollars in 2021. Before this, however, Hormozi said he wasn't happy with his life and felt he was living a path that wasn't his own. Choosing the steps that were true to him "felt like a death decision," he told Steven. "For a period of time I hoped I wouldn't wake up tomorrow. . .and at that time, my father was the most proud of me because I was doing everything according to plan [for how successful I was]."

Hormozi said, "My ultimate expression of living out his dream was feeling like I didn't want to be alive. I realized that one of our dreams had to die, either his or mine, and I kept repeating, 'His dream has to die so that mine can live.'"

That's the paradox: Choosing yourself feels like a funeral before it feels like freedom. Every time we let one dream, expectation, or script die, we create the conditions for our truest self to emerge. The act of choosing yourself is inseparable from the act of choosing hope. One makes space for the other.

Choosing yourself doesn't erase the losses, the betrayals, or the risks. It refuses to let them write your final story. Hope is fragile, yes—but it is also regenerative. It grows back when we dare to believe that tending to our lives is worth the effort, even if we don't know how it will bloom.

That's the first step of living in your True Identity: reclaiming the courage to hope and the audacity to choose yourself. But hope and choice alone won't sustain you. They must be carried, tended, and put to work in the daily soil of your life. That's where stewardship comes in—because what you don't steward, you eventually lose. And your identity is too sacred to lose again.

Friendly Recap

- Hopelessness is your nervous system protecting you, not proof of laziness. Still, if you remain there, that protection can become a cage and lead to choices that increase your suffering instead of lessening it.
- Practice the LIGHT Method. How can you incorporate this into your life once a week? For example, you might take ten minutes on Sunday evening to notice one desire that arose during the week and walk it through the steps. Or do this after coffee with a friend, when their story stirs something in you that feels both hopeful and scary.
- Create a list of no more than three things that you can begin hoping for. Practice this for three weeks, and then slowly increase the level of hope to a risk that feels safe enough to hold. For example, if your hope is for safe connection, send one text or note each week and allow yourself to imagine being received kindly.

Chapter 10

Building Your New Voice

You've outgrown. You've shed. You've released. But the next kind of courage isn't about letting go—it's about *staying who you've become* even when it's misunderstood. This is where your advantage begins: when you stop performing and start protecting what your healing has given you.

Building a house, replanting a tree, remodeling a room—these kinds of re-dos can feel easier, more inviting, and often more rewarding at first than rebuilding ourselves. Tangible progress is easy to spot. You can show it off, snap a photo, or record a time-lapse as another layer gets added. People watching you "ooh" and "ahh" in admiration, moved by what they see taking shape.

But when you begin to build yourself after hardship, the burdens you've carried, or a loss that nearly took your breath away—there aren't any ribbon-cutting ceremonies. There are no housewarming gifts for the soul with handwritten praises for what you've released. Your best friends aren't saying, "I'm proud of you for releasing that vow of 'never again will I.'" More likely, they'll remind you of it: "I thought you said you'd never date again. . . never start another business. . . never have kids." They don't applaud you for trusting others or trusting yourself. The achievement feels silent—no one knows how much it took to speak with your whole voice when shrinking was easier. Family might say, "You've changed." You might get a whole lot *of who the hell does she think she is* energy or *he's gone soft*. People who know you may feel deeply confused and wonder what has happened to you—not because they don't know *what* happened to you, but because they don't understand *how* what happened changed you.

As aggravating as that is, I get it. When we've been a certain way with people over time, they come to know us as that person. If you're always late, they might be surprised the first few times you're on time. If you're historically aggressive and angry, your calmness might be unnerving. If you've always gone with the flow and rarely said no, pushing back or saying no could be shocking.

They expect the old you because that's the only version who has ever shown up. The new you is different. Your new characteristics haven't solidified into patterns or habits yet, so for now, they feel disoriented. And because familiarity breeds *perceived* safety, it's more convenient if you return to who you were than to leave them sitting in the discomfort of your evolution. Therefore, their behavior usually isn't personal. It's not that they don't want you to get better and feel whole; it's that they don't understand what's happening underneath.

It's okay if they don't seem to be happy with the new you. As a True Identity Holder, let the discomfort shift them, not you. Let them meet you here, in the wild place where your life has begun to take root and bloom again. Allow them to adapt to the version of you that's healing. You are not responsible for how others grieve the old version of you. If they aren't content with you taking center stage without a mask, they're welcome to leave the front row.

When Your Healing and Pain Makes Them Uncomfortable

People may criticize you for dreaming "too big," moving to a better neighborhood, applying for the promotion, and disregarding their advice that implies you should stay small. I've rarely met a person who:

- walked in the fullness of their identity who didn't receive criticism.
- allowed themselves to grieve in a healthy way who didn't receive judgment.
- survived hardship without feeling envied, discouraged, or doubted by others.

We confuse being misunderstood with having done something wrong. I say if everyone understands you, you're limiting yourself to what neatly fits in their minds. In Ralph Waldo Emerson's essay "Self-Reliance," he writes, "Is it so bad, then, to be misunderstood? Pythagoras was misunderstood, and Socrates, and Jesus, and Luther, and Copernicus, and Galileo, and Newton, and every pure and wise spirit that ever took flesh. To be great is to be misunderstood."

The Builder Root reframes people's critiques. Criticism is a sign that you are no longer shrinking because people can't judge what they don't see or know about. While shrinking sounds "safe" and seems "good," it'll never get you known as you are for who you are. Criticism is a sign that you're trying, stepping out of the norms; *it's given when your clarity disturbs their comfort, and your discerning heart picks up on their manipulation.* When people benefit from your wounds, your healing becomes inconvenient. It makes them feel the pain they thought they had suppressed; it shines a light on where they need to grow and develop. We only know what an abnormal human cell is because we've studied a healthy one. A person who walks confidently in their identity offers stark contrast to the hard work we must do deep within ourselves.

Examples

The One Who Refuses to Shrink

I used to be an advocate for anyone who was mistreated, but struggled to do so for myself. Gradually, I started increasing my confidence by telling people no and pushing back when their demands or comments weren't appropriate. My friend at the time had made a crude remark to me. I called her out on how she was mistreating me in our friendship and told her that if things did not change, the nature of our friendship would. I'll never forget when she responded with, "I know you've found your voice, but can you dumb down for the rest of us?" Rage overtook me, but I didn't lash out. I said, "I will not make myself small so others can feel big. I will meet people where they are to bring them up, but I won't reduce who I am." She didn't seem to like that response. Soon after that conversation, she told me that our friendship wasn't working anymore. She said, "I don't know who you are anymore," and I was hurt. We had been friends since high school. But the reality was, I wasn't the same person. I was my true self, not a shapeshifting version, and if being me cost me her friendship, it was a price I was willing to pay.

The One Who Speaks Truth

Prince Harry, in public interviews and his book Spare, *described how royal life enforced silence around certain truths. When he spoke honestly about his mother's death and his own struggles, he faced worldwide criticism. Some praised his courage; others mocked him. Within his family, his openness was frowned upon—he no longer felt at home in their system. Sometimes, speaking your truth unsettles those who would rather you stay silent, especially if they've benefited from your compliance.*

The One Who Breaks the Pattern

Marie and Donald were married for eight years. They loved each other deeply but always struggled with decision-making. Donald was indecisive, often defaulting to whatever Marie wanted. He lived by the outdated saying, "Happy wife, happy life." For a while, it seemed to work. Marie enjoyed her freedom, and Donald avoided internal conflict by saying nothing. But after years of never speaking up, Donald began to resent it. Slowly, he started voicing his opinions and reclaiming his agency. While Marie had long asked him to "step up," his newfound assertiveness was unfamiliar and unsettling. It challenged the status quo of their marriage and sparked conflict. Donald's growth disrupted the old dynamic, and Marie struggled to adjust after years of carrying the weight alone.

Criticism Versus Feedback

What is the difference between criticism and feedback? Criticism focuses on what's wrong—perceived or actual. It's often discouraging, demoralizing, and doesn't offer solutions. Feedback, in contrast, highlights someone's challenges alongside their strengths. It's supportive, encouraging, and offers constructive solutions. When someone receives feedback, they don't walk away in shame as they do with criticism. We can help a person improve who they are and how they are without ripping away their dignity, honor, and respect.

But what if I'm the person who tends to criticize others? What if I'm the judgmental one wearing the mask? I remember traveling once and doing a solo hike. I met two women with whom I got into a friendly conversation. One lady looked around, then interrupted and said, "You're alone? You're doing this all by yourself?"

"Yes, it's a good mental break," I told her.

"Oh, I could never. I'd be afraid of what other hikers thought of me, especially those in groups or coupled up."

"I find that most people don't say anything to me," I told her. "Most people are enjoying the hike. Have you looked at a single hiker and thought they must be a loser?"

"Actually, I have," she said. "I'm always thinking, 'Yup, they definitely don't have any friends. Something's wrong with them. Let me stay far away.'" She laughed innocently, and her friend agreed with the statement.

"Well, I guess that makes sense. You fear being judged in the same measure you judge others."

I don't think she liked that comment. And at that point in time, my younger self didn't know how to frame it better.

Both women's faces went blank. One of them tried to force a smile that quickly faded.

"I guess. . .yeah. . .I guess that's right," she said.

As you can imagine, our conversation didn't last much longer after that. The woman thought what held her back from going places alone was others, but realized she was being held back by her own self-criticism.

This is a conversation I introduce to my clients, especially those who join my identity-based groups. We discuss how to give feedback, how to handle it when you're on the receiving side, and what to do when you're criticized. At some point in our sessions, I ask each participant to answer a few questions. I'll offer them to you, as well.

How the Voice Matures as Identity Solidifies

It's important to pause for a moment to check-in with how we feel about someone. It's harder to give constructive feedback when we don't hold someone in positive regard. In the Truth Seeker Root, we talked about how to discern the heart of someone who gives you advice. But roots interweave. Now, in the Builder Root, it's critical to determine *our* heart when offering advice. We do this by asking ourselves a few questions:

- How do I feel toward the person I'm offering feedback to?
- What's motivating me to say this? Is it for my benefit or theirs?
- Have I asked this person if they're open to receiving feedback from me?

Unlike what I did with the women I encountered when hiking, once you ask and receive permission to offer feedback, provide it in this way:

- **Reflect:** Reiterate what you've heard them say. This clarifies that you've understood them correctly, and it confirms that they've been heard. This looks like asking, "What I'm hearing you say is. . ." It also allows for a deeper conversation and correction if any misunderstandings have occurred.

People often hear what they fear, not what was said. Verifying information helps us get the conversation right the first time.

- **Express empathy:** Once you've gained clarity, you can offer kindness. This might sound like:

  "I get why that's hard."
  "That makes so much sense."
  "Thank you for trusting me with that."
  "I can feel how much that meant to you."

  In my situation with the ladies I met hiking, this would have looked like me saying to them, "I can imagine how hiking alone can feel scary, and these days, we put a lot of emphasis on being with people. Walking in the woods by yourself can make us feel physically uncomfortable and maybe question if others see us as 'weird' or 'strange.' I get why you're afraid of judgment."

Empathy doesn't fix the feeling; it gently meets it.

- **Offer feedback:** If the person is open to receiving guidance and suggestions you might ask them more questions—not to catch them, but to free them. Then with their permission, share your feedback. You can also share any observed positive attributes and strengths. We say, "No news is good news," but this sets the expectation that feedback comes when something is wrong. The result? Commentary feels like criticism, not recognition. Instead, make it a habit to offer praise when things are going well. When people feel seen for their everyday goodness, they become more open to opinions. Building a culture of everyday appreciation lays the groundwork for trust and honest dialogue when tensions arise. When people understand you see the good in them, they can properly frame your requests for improvement. By naming the beauty first they are more likely to trust you with what's "ugly." They lean in rather than leaving and receive what you've said without pushing against it.

This would have looked like me offering praise to the woman, "It's great that you're outdoors and decided to hike with a friend. Something stood out to me when you mentioned judging solo hikers. Is it okay to share my thoughts on that?"

On Receiving Feedback

- If the person asked me if I wanted feedback, was I honest with my "yes"? I might be less receptive if I've falsely given them permission.
- If the person is offering unsolicited advice, have I thanked them for trying to help and made them aware I'm not open to this form of support right now?

When it comes to understanding if what they are saying is true or applicable, use discernment. Feel welcome to return to the Truth Seeker Root to practice these skills.

A Gentle Note: Feedback Is a Gift

Keep in mind that feedback is a gift. It allows you to see your blind spots, improve, and acquire wisdom you didn't have to pay for with tears, lost gains, or hardships. Being able to receive this from others shows your commitment to improving, living more from who you are, and an openness to receive from others. It strengthens your relationships when people can pour into you and be a support in who you're becoming after such great loss—even if they aren't aware of the full story.

The Voice Ladder

Most people think you either speak up or stay silent. But it's more nuanced than that. When rebuilding identity, we often move through four voice styles (more on that later). What we want our words to be heard through is the **True Identity Voice**, the steady, rooted way you speak when you know who you are. It's calm without shrinking, assertive without being cruel, and direct without apologizing. Your Identity Voice doesn't overexplain, perform, or chase permission. It's not about being liked; it's about becoming someone *you* love. It's about being true to yourself, your values, and others.

You might still be forming this voice and learning how to put language to your thoughts, body sensations, and emotions. And this might confuse others. Remember, that despite *our* knowing we are changing into someone new, others *aren't* aware of this yet. It takes time, repetition, and consistency to build a new pattern from the self *we've* previously created.

People expect what they have always gotten—including your Shapeshifter Voice.

For us to understand how to develop our True Identity Voice, we must first understand how we currently speak. There are four dominant communication styles: passive, passive aggressive, aggressive, and assertive. Understanding which you default to is important because as you transform internally, your skills should reflect your new identity externally. Contrary to what we often believe, it's not always our grief and pain that turn people off; it's the way we communicate. Sometimes we are the ones creating conflict, inviting frustration or manipulation, or pushing people away because of *how* we deliver *our* message.

Unclear communication confuses people, disengages them, and impedes connection, intimacy, and support. The good news is ineffective communication isn't a fixed issue or a diagnosis. Many of us inherit our patterns from family members and those around us. Because verbal expression is learned, we can unlearn what isn't working and develop skills that will best benefit us and our relationships.

As you read through these four voices, consider the following:

- Which voice represents the old you?
- Which voice represents the present-day you?
- Which voice do you want to evolve into?

The Passive Communicator

This style avoids conflict at all costs. It downplays needs, suppresses discomfort, and gives up time, energy, or voice to preserve peace. There are myriad reasons for why we might fall into this form of communication. Maybe it's what was modeled in our childhood, it feels safer based on our situations or our natural temperament, or we were raised to "play nice." At the root is a fear of what will happen should we speak up for ourselves. We see this illustrated in the following story.

Aviva didn't mind meeting for brunch. She liked the way the light hit the windows at Stella's Café, and Neela always had stories to tell. But lately, their hangouts started to feel more like emotional labor than connection.

Neela was mid-story before Aviva had taken off her coat.

"So, then he says he *needs space*, right after telling me he wants to work things out. And work's been nonstop. I swear, I feel like I'm holding everybody together."

Aviva nodded and gripped her hands around her coffee.

Before Aviva could respond, Neela said, "And then my sister. It's ridiculous. I was with her yesterday and could you believe. . ."

It only took five minutes for Aviva to regret meeting up with her friend. Her original plan for the weekend was to rest. She had been going nonstop at work and home, and doing nothing sounded wonderful. But Aviva struggled with saying no. When they had finished lunch, Aviva internally sighed. *Whew, I can go home now.*

But Neela had other plans. "Can we stop by my house after this? I need help hanging my new TV, and I know you're great with stuff like that."

"Sure. . .that's fine," Aviva said reluctantly. *So much for having a relaxing weekend.* The ladies grabbed the check and headed to the parking lot.

The drive to Neela's was quiet—at least from Aviva's side. Neela did most of the talking, as she continued on about her ex, her family, and work. Aviva stared out the window, tuning out the words and feeling the ache in her temples. Her body had been asking for rest all week. She hadn't listened. She rarely did.

When they pulled into the driveway, Neela turned to her and smiled. "Thanks again. I know I ask for a lot sometimes."

Aviva shook her head. "No, it's okay."

Inside, Neela laid out the tools and walked into the kitchen, talking over her shoulder about dinner plans. Aviva stood there alone, staring at the blank wall where the TV was supposed to go, unsure of how she'd gotten here *again*. Not here as in Neela's house, but here—overextended, exhausted, and disappearing by degrees.

After the TV was up, Neela called from the kitchen, "Do you want to stay for dinner? I'm making that pasta you like."

Aviva groaned inside. She didn't want pasta. She didn't want to talk. She didn't want to be here. She wanted to go home hours ago. But she'd already said yes so many times today, what was one more? "Sure," she said.

After dinner, the two ladies cleaned up, chatting a bit more, until finally, it was late enough for Aviva to feel she could call it quits. She hugged her friend, grabbed her purse, and headed out to go home. Except later that night, soon after her head hit the pillow, her phone rang. It was another friend calling. Aviva was exhausted; she had nothing left. *I'm tired of being the go-to support person.* After a minute or two she realized she missed Julia's call. She sighed, braced herself, then proceeded to call her back.

When Aviva went to speak to her therapist, she told him, "All of my friends take advantage of me. It's always about them: what they like and what they want to do."

While that narrative was her perceived truth, the reality of her experience wasn't so. Aviva never pushed back or made herself unavailable. She treated her boundaries as suggestions, and even then, the line between where her boundaries started and ended was unknown because she never voiced them. Aviva was going to therapy to heal, and likely did make some improvements, but her passive communication style kept her stuck in a cycle. And from there, she based life—and people—on how she felt.

She expected people to "just know" what she needed and act upon it, despite her knowing and not acting upon it herself. The resentment she felt, the anger, became misplaced. It wasn't her friends who ignored her needs, it was Aviva undermining Aviva's needs. Because she didn't address her fear of speaking up, her challenges worsened.

Psychologist Randy J. Paterson proposed that "people who rely exclusively on the passive style really are helpless because they can't override the demands of others. As a result, the helplessness may escalate into discouragement, a sense of futility, or even all-out depression."[1]

Gentle Note

Many people who communicate passively think they're being "nice." But niceness without truth isn't safety. It's disconnection. People don't know where you stand, so those who mean well can't fully support you. Healthy people want to hear your opinions and want you to share in decision-making. They don't want relationships with people who always want to please them or

[1] Randy, J. (2022). *Paterson, The Assertiveness Workbook*, 2nde, 15. Oakland, CA: New Harbinger Publications.

aren't true to themselves. They might be turned off by it and shift the relationship accordingly. It is hard to trust someone when they almost always agree with you—it comes off as disingenuous, and healthy people can discern this. They want to respect you, but it's hard to figure this out unless you state what makes you feel respected. For those who have entered your life only to misuse you, they benefit from you not advocating for yourself. Staying in a state of passive communication can prolong their mistreatment of you.

The Passive Aggressive Communicator

Passive-aggressive communicators also fear being direct about their needs or feelings. But rather than staying silent or compliant, they use a different approach—like Sour Patch Kids candy: sweet at first, then suddenly sour. It's the jab dressed as a joke. The compliment wrapped around critique. A delay disguised as forgetfulness.

At its core, this style is about control. It's resentment with its shapeshifting mask on. There's often anger underneath, but instead of expressing it directly, this communicator avoids confrontation, then punishes people in subtle ways. Not because they don't care, but because they're scared that if they say what they feel, they'll be judged, abandoned, or seen as "not enough or too much."

Some of this is learned behavior. The thinking goes: *If I can't say how I really feel, I'll hint. If I can't say no, I'll delay. If I can't be heard, I'll go quiet and make you guess.*

But here's the hard truth: Healthy people don't want to guess. They don't want to decode. They honor the distance you create and assume you mean what you say. If you tell them, *I'm fine,* they won't question you because they respect boundaries. And if you avoid them, they won't become desperate for your attention. That is not because they don't care; it's because they do. They are walking in their True Identity, and they understand that manipulating you to stay or speak up is *not* a form of love.

As you've consistently learned, with each of these foundations our behaviors are driven by what makes *us* feel safe. Therefore, like other learned behaviors and coping strategies, we don't shame this form of communication. Passive–aggressive behavior is rooted in abandonment and rejection wounds. It sounds like: *I want to tell you I'm upset, but I'm scared you'll leave. So instead, I'll joke about it. I'll do what you asked, then resent you for it and blow up in anger and disappointment.*

This is especially common for those who have experienced prolonged trauma, grief, and hardship. Their voice became the storage room for everything they never got to say, causing anger to leak sideways in tone, sarcasm, or withdrawal. It sounds like, *I don't even know who or what I'm mad about anymore.* That's the grief talking, the accumulated exhaustion and overwhelm. It's what happens when hope becomes misplaced.

Love isn't proven by how well someone can read your silence. It's revealed in how safely you can bring your truth to the table.

Let's Continue with Our Story

It was Saturday afternoon, and Aviva pulled into her parents' driveway. They were having their monthly family get together, the grand ol' Kaplan dinner. Aviva hated these; they weren't fun, but her parents insisted. Aviva and her three other siblings each traveled an hour for them to be together.

When she walked in the house, her mom embraced her with a hug and kiss, but Aviva let her arms dangle to her side with a "Hi, mom," as she walked away. She half-smiled at her father who, preoccupied with his phone and the sports game on TV, lifted his pointer finger as his signature wave. Aviva plopped down on the couch opposite him, and she heard her siblings arguing as they came toward the room.

Dad looked over at them, "Well, well, look who showed up. If it's not Micah. How's the job going down at the deli, son? Have you made enough to buy your nametag yet?"

Oh, there he goes. He couldn't resist knocking Micah down again, knowing he's already struggling, Aviva thought.

Micah walked away with his head down when Hannah, their oldest sister, entered holding apple pie.

"Mom asked us to bring dessert," Hannah said, setting the dish on the table. "But don't worry, Aviva, I covered for you."

"Awe, thanks Hannah," Aviva said, "You saved me from being the family's disappointment once again."

Their mom popped in from the kitchen, drying her hands on a towel. "Girls, let's not start."

Start? Did she not hear what Hannah said? Aviva thought. *I knew I should have stayed home.*

Dinner moved on, and conversations spun from person to person. Hannah's new yoga certification, Micah's latest date stories, Mom's neighbor drama. The smell of garlic filled the air—there was always too much garlic in the green beans. Mom insisted it was the Kaplan's most prized "tradition." No one had the heart to tell her it'd probably taste better with less.

"So, Aviva," her dad said between bites, "you dating anyone yet or are you planning for your first kid to think you're the grandma?"

Aviva's fork clinked a little too hard against her plate. She swallowed. "Oh, I'm just waiting for someone as great as my father," she said. "You know, a guy who calls me once a month to insult my life choices."

The rest of the siblings snickered, and dad looked angry.

"How about we talk about why we're grateful to be here together?" Mom suggested. "I think that's a fabulous idea. Don't you think?"

Everyone mumbled. "I'm actually done with my dinner," one sibling said getting up from the table. "Yeah, it's late, I need to get back on the road," said another. Micah looked around and said, "Me too. I have to work extra hours tomorrow, to afford my name tag, you know."

Aviva saw this as an opportunity to leave, but when her mom asked her to stay behind to clean up with Hannah, she grabbed the dishes in anger.

"Everything okay?" her mom asked.

"Yup. I'm fine. Everything here is normal," Aviva said, before mumbling "as usual" underneath her breath.

Why Building New Patterns Is Hard

For Aviva, shedding her passive, and sometimes passive-aggressive, communication style came with obstacles. For one, it was hard to see that anything was wrong with how she spoke to people—her family thrived on it. Taking jabs and speaking with harshness was normal. *It's hard to change a problem you don't know you have.* It was like mom's green beans: everyone thought the family tradition would be better off with less garlic, but no one spoke up. They thought their honesty would break her heart, not the lies they told.

Extra layers of difficulty are added when there aren't any contrasting models of how conversations could be different. For Aviva, she could almost argue that being passive and passive-aggressive helped her survive being in her family's environment. When people fear being close, passive-aggressive communication is used to create emotional distance.

It's likely that their father was frustrated with how his children's lives were going. Maybe he expected better of them, believed they had more potential, or felt they were wasting their time away. Regardless of the reason, making snide remarks wasn't going to get them there any faster, at least not without damaging their self-esteem or parent-to-child relationship.

What would it have cost Hannah to offer to teach her sister a recipe? Or Aviva to say what she really wanted—for her dad to call her more often? The intent behind what each person did was present, but the way they spoke to each other never reflected it. Instead, it was demeaning, destructive, and created a space where conflict was the only way they could connect with one another. And yet, it was that shared characteristic that made them dread staying at dinner and excited to leave.

As you look into your own life, does the way you communicate with anyone look like this? Do you use passive-aggressive language toward those you'd like to have a good relationship with? What does distancing yourself accomplish that you're afraid being honest about your feelings won't?

Here are a few examples. For more scripts, visit theidentityresetbook.com/bookextras

Passive Aggressive Response	**Healthy Assertive Response**
"I'm fine." (But withdraws, sulks.)	"I'm hurt by what happened, and I'd like to talk about it."
"Wow, must be nice to never help with the dishes." (Jokes about being upset.)	"I feel overwhelmed when I do the dishes alone. Could you help me more regularly?"
"Sure, I'll do it. I'm usually the one who does." (Then complains.)	"I can't take that on right now. Could we find another solution together?"

The Aggressive Communicator

We think aggressive communication is about dominance or ego, but that's only because it's misunderstood. Beneath the fiery tones, the yelling, and the anger is someone who holds fear, survival, and aloneness. The aggressive communicator has a history of their own. Many either witnessed this form of communication in their upbringing or found it immediately gratifying after using it.

For others, they didn't start out aggressive. They tried being calm, patient, and vulnerable, but after being ignored and minimized, aggression became the only response people heard. Their rage stems from years of trying nicely, feeling unsafe, and getting nowhere.

So, while we interpret the aggressive person as mean or angry—and they are—what they might feel is a repeated violations of their boundaries, the injustice of how they've been treated, and the sad reality that the only way to have some form of respect is by intimidating and controlling others.

Grief and life changes can make us sad, but they also have the power to alter how we speak. Some of us go silent, or we switch along the way. Maybe you've noticed your tone of voice softening or feeling clunky or loud. That's not a flaw. It's a signal of deeper hurt. Let's talk about what happens when pain turns to aggression.

Back to Aviva. . .

Aviva sat on the edge of the couch in her therapist's office. She barely budged and kept her arms crossed.

"I'm tired," she said. "I'm tired of being the one who's always understanding. Giving the benefit of the doubt. The go-to person for everybody else's emotional crisis."

Her therapist frowned, sharing in Aviva's sadness.

"Neela? She wants me to hang out again this weekend. She said she needs help processing her breakup. *Again*. And my family?" Aviva said. "Last Sunday was a circus. Micah stormed off after Dad made a low-ball comment, mom acted like nothing happened—as usual—and I got left cleaning up with Hannah."

"That is—" the therapist said, as Aviva interrupted.

"If they would go to therapy—and fix their issues, then I could finally have some peace! But, oh, no! Everyone wants to call Aviva! Why can't they figure it out themselves and leave me alone?!"

Her therapist paused. "It makes sense that you're tired. You're carrying a lot. It's valid to want peace, and to want others to take responsibility for their behavior."

Aviva nodded, eyes wide, waiting for the next validation, but what came next was unexpected.

"I wonder, Aviva, if we could also explore what role you might have in contributing to these persisting patterns."

"Excuse me?"

"Not that it's your fault," her therapist said gently. "But I wonder if there are any ways, subconsciously so, that you've helped the cycles continue."

Aviva leaned forward and pointed to her chest. "You think *I'm* the problem?"

"No, you are *not* the problem. I am saying you're part of the dynamic. Think of it like tug-of-war. Both you and the other people are pulling the rope. That means both are participating in the push-and-pull relationship."

Aviva laughed sarcastically. "Right. *So*, let me get this straight. They make jabs, guilt-trip me, dump their emotions on me, and I'm supposed to do a self-inventory about *my* part?! What type of therapist are you?! You sound just like them! *'What did you do to cause it?' 'Maybe you misunderstood.' 'You're too sensitive.'* I came here for support! Not to be gaslit by someone with a license!" Aviva screamed and her fists pounded into the couch. "You're going to screw me over and throw jabs like everyone else!"

The room lost its sound.

Like a bad phone connection that echoes your own voice, Aviva heard hers in the silence. Her chest rose and fell with each breath, and for a second, she looked like a deer in headlights—except this time, she herself was the approaching object. Tucked behind her words was the pain of being unseen, unheard, and alone. This wasn't about her, but the therapist neither retaliated nor defended himself.

"Aren't you upset that I'm angry?" Aviva asked.

"No," the therapist said calmly. "I *care* about you being angry. I'm *not* upset by it. You sharing what hurts, what you find frustrating, is healthy. It can mean you feel safe enough to push back—to tell me no, to speak up for yourself."

Aviva gave a slight nod and a brief exhale.

"What was that like?" Her therapist asked. "To be angry and say how you felt?"

"Well, I'm not sure if all of that was true." Aviva hunched over and broke eye contact.

"Hmm. . .what if we don't focus on what's true or isn't right now. What was it like to feel angry, to not like what someone—well, what I said, and tell me how you felt? To say, 'No, that's not okay,' and release it?"

"I feel like no one hears me or cares." Aviva was deflecting from answering the *right* question—the one about how speaking up felt. It was likely unintentional, but subconsciously, perhaps scary to acknowledge.

She shifted in her chair, then rubbed her hands together. Her foot tapped, she made eye contact with the therapist, then looked away, only to repeat the process. "I feel bad. But, I guess it also felt good to say how I felt." She said it with a smile so slight, most would have missed it.

Power Gained and Lost

Aggression isn't always about overpowering others—it's often an attempt to reclaim the self-agency you've lost. But when we don't feel safe, we can overcorrect. What starts as a cry for dignity ends in an attack. Aggression may get people's attention, but it won't respectfully keep it.

Despite what many say, anger is not a "negative" emotion. Anger matters, not being fairly treated or unheard matters. However, we have to be careful how we use anger. For Aviva, the person she released years of rage toward, her therapist, was someone who understood how to navigate this type of situation. But most people aren't therapists. This could have easily started a fight, an argument, or resulted in a situation that would be hard to forget. And all for what? Because Aviva's true fear—of feeling bad for speaking up—is what needed to be held.

Crappy situations might have happened to you. Like Aviva, you likely didn't choose to yell—you evolved into it. This also means transformation is possible. Anger doesn't have to be your forever go-to way of communicating. Healing won't mute you or cause you to *never* raise your voice. It means learning how to use it without losing yourself, and your true message, in the process.

The Assertive Communicator

The fourth style, assertiveness, is what we're all told to aim for but rarely taught how to embody. Assertive communication isn't about being loud or confident all the time. It's not about always having the perfect words or sounding polished. It's being rooted—in your needs, your values, and your self-respect. Assertive communication says: *Here's what I believe. Here's what I need. And here's what I'm available for and what I'm not.*

It's direct without being cold, kind without being passive, firm without being cruel. Unless this form of communication was modeled in your upbringing, many do not build their assertive, Identity Voice by skipping over pain. They get there by walking through it, most often, after all the other ways haven't worked: not saying anything, half-way voicing their opinions, exploding too often, or "forgetting" their needs exist.

Assertiveness is the fruit that grows after your roots have gone deep, when you know who you are, what you stand for, and you stop performing to avoid your inner discomfort. That's the season Aviva found herself in. The Builder Root helped her develop her unique sound. Let's see what that looks like for her.

Aviva's True Identity Voice

After that last therapy session—Aviva realized she had put too much blame on others for how her conversations played out. Sure, she couldn't change people, but for those who were willing to change, she hadn't given them a chance. Aviva left that session thinking, *What if other people can respond to me like my therapist? Especially if I'm not rude about what I need or how I feel? Maybe I wouldn't be as angry because they'd see me. And if they don't, then, I don't have to wonder if they will. I know where I stand.*

A month or two later, and after several therapy sessions, she met Neela at their usual spot. Neela was already sipping her oat milk latte and scrolling her phone.

"Hey," Aviva said, sliding into the seat across from her.

Neela smiled, "Hey. Thanks for meeting. I've had the craziest week. I need to vent."

"Before we jump in—can I share something first?"

Neela blinked, surprised. "Sure. What's up?"

Aviva took a breath. Her heart was racing fast. Thoughts of making up a different story to tell came to mind, but she was also tired of breaking promises to herself about what she would say this time and next.

"I've noticed something about our friendship," Aviva said. "I love being someone you can talk to. I really do. But sometimes, it feels like I'm your therapist, not your friend. And I've been realizing how drained I feel after we hang out."

Neela's face dropped a little. "Oh."

"I'm not mad," Aviva said. "But I can't do a vent session today."

"Okay, that's cool." Neela said unbothered.

Aviva looked shocked. *That's it?*

"Why didn't you say something before? I always wondered why you were quiet. Thanks for letting me know."

Aviva wasn't sure if she trusted Neela to not respond like this every time, but she was glad her friend was receptive. She knew she had a long way to go. There was still her family's Sunday dinner. She had to build more confidence to speak up around them. But she figured she'd start out small, with safer people like Neela, and one day, hopefully gain the courage and practice to let the Builder Root show up elsewhere—in her community and her Identity Voice.

Start Where It's Safe

Just because you change doesn't mean others want to, will, or should. That's a tough truth, when you're growing into your true self. As cliché as it sounds, "birds of a feather flock together" rings true. As your communication improves, you may notice what others' communication styles are, not in a way that judges, but in a way that discerns.

You might also notice that your Identity Voice contrasts against theirs. While assertiveness comes with clarity, kindness, and directness, others might not receive it well at first. It can feel sharp to them because it isn't what they are used to from you. It's normal for people to misread your assertiveness as rudeness if they don't feel comfortable with someone who voices their needs, boundaries, or speaks truth.

Others might brace for the usual misunderstanding with you, but it's now absent. They're still expecting the old pattern, and that's okay. If we're super honest with ourselves (thanks Truth Seeker Root), we'd likely respond the same way. Be patient—with yourself *and* them. They likely need as much time to adjust as you do.

Like Aviva, change usually starts small. When you've spent years speaking from a shape-shifting voice, it makes sense that reclaiming your true one takes time. Begin with people who you feel safer with—this offers quicker wins and less risk. Being assertive with strangers at the grocery store, while on the phone with customer service, and when you speak to people in passing are all great starts. Sometimes it's easier to practice with people you'll likely never see again. It reduces the pressure to "get it right" and the fear of them not speaking to you again.

Lastly, if you're in a relationship, or have people you feel close enough to share your journey with, it might be helpful to tell them, "Hey, I'm working on my communication skills. If I sound a little different lately, that's why." Are they owed this? No, but a heads-up gives them context instead of confusion.

If you're lucky, they'll rise to meet you in your Identity Reset. When growth looks good on you, others get curious about what life would be like if they stepped out of their shape-shifting identity, too.

Review: The Identity Behind Each Style

Style	Core Identity Beliefs
Passive	– "My needs don't matter." – "I'll be rejected if I speak up." – "It's safer to stay small or go unnoticed."
Passive-Aggressive	– "If I say it directly, I'll be punished or ignored." – "People don't care about my feelings, so I'll protect myself." – "I have to hint at my pain because I can't trust others with it."
Aggressive	– "No one protects me, so I have to protect myself." – "I only get taken seriously when I'm angry." – "Being vulnerable is dangerous—it gets used against me."
Assertive	– "My needs matter, and so do yours." – "I can speak my truth without harming myself or others." – "I know who I am, and I no longer need to prove it through performance."

The Builder Root Builds Your Voice

A common piece of current advice says, "You need to find your voice." After going through my upheaval of defeats, losses, and uphill battles, I realized why it never sat well with me. We don't find our voice. We create it—like a musician creates their own sound. Maybe it's the inner child musician in me, but I equate my voice to an instrument.

We're using what's already there. We learn the language of sound, through reading notes, playing by ear, or a general gut feeling. Once we've learned, you know what we do? We create a song. We play. In his Oscar acceptance speech for the film *Soul*, composer Jon Batiste talked about how everyone has the same musical language, but what makes it different is how it is used. He said, "It's the same twelve notes that Duke Ellington had, that Bach had, Nina Simone, it's the same twelve! Every gift is special. Every contribution with music that comes from the divine into the instruments, into the film, into the minds and hearts and souls of every person who hears it, the stories that happen when you listen to it and watch it and the stories you share, the moments you create, the memories you make. . .man, it's just so incredibly special."

We are no different. We each have language, and individually we are using it express our identity in a way that brings harmony to us and others. If we were to liken your identity voice to music, it'd appear as:

- **Tuning** = Becoming emotionally aware before speaking.
- **Tempo** = Pacing your message. (Don't rush. Don't freeze.)
- **Volume** = Choosing tone, not just words.
- **Practice** = Every conversation is rehearsal for the next.
- **Song Choice** = You decide which people to share your "music" with.

As the "composer" of your True Identity, you get to be the author, narrator, and the main character. You get to choose who you want to share the song with—your community—and weed out those who are consistently offbeat and out of tune with this version of who you are. The musician doesn't get on stage and apologize for how he played his song. Neither should you.

Your voice grows each time you choose to use it with intention. With every conversation, boundary, question, and moment of clarity, you're shaping a sound that carries who you really are. Let your voice belong to you again, and as it strengthens, you'll notice something beautiful: The people who are meant for this version of you will recognize it, respond to it, and rise alongside you.

Friendly Recap

- Your voice grows as your identity grows. Every boundary, pause, honest sentence, and moment of self-respect is part of building a new pattern. *You're not "finding" your voice—you're creating one that reflects who you've become, not who you had to be.*
- Old dynamics don't determine your future conversations. Whether you were passive, passive–aggressive, aggressive, or unclear, these were survival strategies—not character flaws. As your Identity Voice matures, you get to choose new ways of communicating that honor both you and the people in front of you.
- Start where it feels safest. Practicing your new voice doesn't have to begin with the hardest relationships. Begin with the low-risk spaces, the people who can receive you, and the moments where authenticity feels possible. Every practiced moment strengthens your capacity to speak from who you truly are. Where in your life (or with whom) are you being invited to use your truest voice next, and what would it sound like if you trusted it?

Chapter 11

Building Your Community

While many have written about the importance of community, I've found that trauma survivors don't need more people—they need *the right roles* in their life. That's why I developed the Three Builders framework. Because having friends, mentors, and a strong community is the cheat sheet to feeling well loved, wanted, and protected. Yet, what comes to mind when you hear the phrase "you need community?" Does that sound like a lot of people? A part of life you feel you're better off without, struggling to have, or satisfied in? It's extremely common for those who have experienced life transitions, immense grief, and losses to lack the connections they need.

The loss of friendships, the shifting of others, and the family members who fade away or aren't sure how to support you are all a natural part of experiencing change. It doesn't feel good when this happens and can become yet another loss to process on top of everything else you're carrying. While you might feel like you're the only one going through what you're facing, you aren't. There is a community of people who will stand by your side. It might not seem like it, and perhaps you've had unfavorable connections until now. However, as you walk into your True Identity, you'll encounter people who are willing to invest in your present journey.

Recognizing these people is easier than you thought, too. That's because most of us only need three close people in our inner circle. I refer to them as the **Three Builders**—the person who protects you, the person who guides you, and the person who offers love. Each one supports a psychological need: safety, clarity, and love and belonging. If you position each of these people in your life correctly, you will feel nourished and transformed by them. Misplace them, and unnecessary strain and tension might appear. So, let's begin by breaking down who each of these builders are.

Builder One: The Protector

A protective person keeps you safe when your boundaries get blurry, your internal and psychological world feel uneasy, and the people around you forget to hold you without harming you. Yes, this person is here in good times, but they are especially helpful when we struggle to safeguard ourselves. The Protector looks out for you when your identity is fragile by helping you feel safe to exist.

Their Position in Your Community

This person won't always know what to say, but they'll show up when it counts. Allow this person to step in when you feel unsafe or life feels too big to handle alone.

This Relationship Shines When

- You need someone to advocate for your needs.
- You're left in a vulnerable state after loss and need someone to watch out for you.
- You need someone whose presence brings safety to the room.

Characteristics of the Protector

- They are motivated by loyalty to you.
- They aren't always emotionally nuanced but remain supportive.
- They are passionate about what's sacred to you.

A Word of Caution

The Protector's strength isn't in being silent or gentle. This is the person you go to when you need someone to be a defender on your behalf, not to provide comfort or validation. Feeling deeply *might* not be a strength of theirs.

What the Protector Looks Like

Naomi was at her job for two years when a fellow colleague, Mary, started mistreating her. After several attempts to address Mary's behavior, Naomi realized something more needed to be done. But Naomi was scared. In her old identity, she tended to avoid conflict and allow people to treat her like a doormat. Speaking up for her needs and wants and how she deserved to be treated was new. Naomi had befriended another coworker, Rosie, who was assertive in nature and well respected. When she confided in Rosie how she was being treated, Rosie encouraged Naomi to speak up.

"You should take this to human resources. The verbal abuse is rude and demeaning," Rosie said to Naomi. "If you'd like, I'll go with you. I've witnessed how she is toward you. I don't mind being a support."

The two women went together to HR, and when Naomi struggled to fully advocate for herself, Rosie stepped in. She stood by her colleague's side, offered her statement in the written report, and ensured that Naomi wasn't brushed off when explaining what was happening to her.

Who's in Your Circle?

Begin evaluating the people in your life. Do you see anyone who naturally steps into this role? If not, that's okay! As you continue to develop your identity and meet new people, notice if you encounter people who embody the characteristics of the Protector.

Builder Two: The Guide

It's rare for anyone to escape survival mode—let alone thrive beyond it—without the presence of a Guide. Whether in stories or real life, transformation is often accelerated through mentorship. Beethoven had Haydn. Cinderella had the Fairy Godmother. Bilbo had Gandalf. Steve Jobs mentored Zuckerberg. Dr. Benjamin E. Mays poured into Dr. King. Their greatness didn't arise in isolation; it was shaped and sharpened through trusted counsel.

As minister Jerry Flowers Jr. wisely said, "Wisdom is a scholarship. You get to go for free because someone else already paid the cost."[1] Life is too short to learn every lesson the hard way. And yet, many of us do—ignoring insight, resisting counsel, choosing to pay the full price for a lesson someone

---

[1] TikTok - Make Your Day. (n.d.). https://www.tiktok.com/@jerryflowers.jr/video/7082542127586004266#:~:text=%23destinydecisions,to%20make%20my%20decision%20right?

was willing to give us for free. The goal isn't to do it alone. The goal is to learn and seek wise counsel.

And while we may receive many guides in our lives, there's usually one person who is monumental. We encounter them at the crossroads—when we're unsure how to move from who we were to who life is asking us to be. In the Releaser Root, we talked about how each of us holds a hidden treasure, but it's guarded by a dragon. The Guide is the builder who shows you how to face the dragon—not with fear or force, but with wisdom. They teach you how to reach your treasure without getting burned, further bruised, or wasting energy you can't afford to sacrifice.

Their Position in Your Community

This is your trusted advisor. Their role isn't always proximity, it's perspective. When you need clarity or recalibration, this is who you turn to.

> *True support doesn't leave you exposed in your vulnerability; it covers you with its protection.*

This Relationship Shines When

- You're lacking clarity or need a trusted second opinion.
- You need someone to reflect your strengths and point out patterns that need improvement.
- You need someone who offers insight without trying to control or "fix" you.

Characteristics of the Guide

- They have high discernment and can hold complexity and nuance.
- They offer gentle truth, without ego, and take joy in guiding others.

- They are willing to pause and consider all the details before speaking.

A Word of Caution

The Guide has the best for you in mind. They'll lovingly offer a new lens, and one that comes without shame and judgment. They may not cradle your pain in their palms, but they'll teach you how to carry it without collapsing.

What the Guide Looks Like

A few weeks after Jason died, my aunt came to my house and found me in the bed crying, miserable and alone. I was devastated and felt like no one understood me. My Aunt Glen talked to me for a moment and offered comforting words. Then, she recommended a change of scenery.

"Let's go out," she said. "It's a nice day out. Get out of bed."

"No, I'm staying inside. I'm too sad."

"Would you rather cry in a Bentley or cry at the bus stop?" she asked me.

I looked at her with confusion. Both of us had cars, and neither were Bentleys.

"Listen, Ashley, life is a ride. Right now, you're at the bus stop. If we go out, you can cry in the Bentley. It might not change how you feel, but it makes the ride better."

I've named this moment "The Bentley or the Bus Stop" and have since shared it with friends, clients, and strangers along the way. More importantly, I remind myself of it. The Guide can be someone who holds you accountable, advises you in business, or how to potty train your child. They can also be someone who offers you a perspective you hadn't considered. Be it a tender suggestion, such as my aunt gave, or a concrete recommendation, they show you what's in your power to change.

Who's in Your Circle?

What leaders or mentors do you have in your life? Remember that your three builders can be anyone—a coworker, teacher, relative, or someone else you've met along the way. As you evaluate your life, who is willing to be honest with you about you? A true Guide is rare, but if you're willing to receive what they carry, you don't need many. As you connect with the treasure inside of you, be on the lookout for those who are willing to guide you.

Builder Three: The Loving One

If you're feeling down and out, and simply need a moment to exhale, the Loving One is who you reach out for and isn't necessarily a romantic partner. It is someone who loves you completely, for who you are, as you are. In the initial seasons of loss and life changes, this person soothes the soul in ways few can. Their purpose is to be a gentle and consistent presence that reminds you of how worthy you are to be loved. When you feel unseen or too fragmented to connect with yourself and others, the Loving One wraps you in empathy and compassion.

You don't need to "do" anything to be in receipt of their love and kindness. This person appreciates and honors your presence and your ability to show up as you are. When we feel safe with someone—like with a Loving Builder—our nervous system can move from survival to regulation. That's not just emotional, it's biological. Their presence helps our body unlearn what hardship taught it.

Their Position in Your Community

The Loving One is the person you place close to your heart. You allow yourself to safely communicate how you feel—the sorrows and the joys. This person is safe to confide in and will hold what you say with respect and confidence.

This Relationship Shines When

- You've lost someone (or something) that made you feel known, and the emptiness feels unbearable.
- You're in a season where you don't need to be "talked at," only sat with.
- You're exploring who you are without a role, title, relationship, or label and feel like nothing is left.

Characteristics of the Loving One

- They are emotionally grounded and safe.
- They feel comfortable with presence over solutions.
- The offer devotion, validation, and reassurance.

A Word of Caution

The Loving One may not be the one to guide or protect. Don't demand direction or defense—let their love be enough.

What the Loving One Looks Like

Jasmine was a young mother whose twins died because of a miscarriage. She was a strong, healthy person and couldn't fathom why, despite following the doctor's orders for a successful pregnancy, her chances of having children ended. Many people around her comforted her at first, but then followed up with comments such as, "You can have another baby" or "At least it wasn't like an adult kid who died." Some even made religious comments such as, "God needed the babies more" and "Heaven had a different plan for your life." These remarks only made Jasmine feel more isolated and dismissed.

As the weeks and months passed, relatives and friends asked her if she was "trying again." Older women gave her tips on how to have a better pregnancy, and none of it felt helpful. However, Jasmine had one friend, Janiah, who checked in on her daily. She'd provide Jasmine with comfort, reminding her that the miscarriage wasn't a result of her having failed. She encouraged her that it was okay to be sad, and asked if she had names for the twins, or if it felt comfortable to name them.

Janiah recognized that her friend had not only lost two babies, but also the opportunity to be a mom to them in years to come. She acknowledged that "trying again" wasn't what Jasmine would have ever wanted. Having children and raising them well was. For Jasmine, Janiah's presence brought relief. It felt soothing to be seen without being fixed, to be allowed to speak about what hurt without being rushed to silence or solutions. With Janiah, grief didn't have to be justified. It was honored.

Who's in Your Circle?

Have you met any Janiahs in your life? Perhaps they start out as small interactions: the stranger who shows you kindness, the therapist who offers support, the person in your hobby group who hangs out after the meeting to listen to you. There are more Janiahs than we can imagine, especially as we become open to receiving support and care. Take inventory of your relationships and see who might fit this role.

A Note on Loss

If you are grieving the loss of someone who was among your Three Builders, building community can cause sadness. I understand, especially as someone who has been widowed twice. My Loving One was found within them. It's difficult when the one person who can make us feel better is the one whom we are grieving most. Be gentle with your heart and kind to your mind. It might be hard connecting with this third builder because no one can replace the person who has died. Remember, you don't have to rush this process. If this part of the chapter feels like it presses on your grief, let your heart ache. Let your love for them rise. You are not being asked to replace them. You're being invited to receive care again when you are ready.

What Kind of Builder Are You?

Consider which builder you are for those around you. Many people find that they may shift among the three but have a dominant characteristic. For example, perhaps you are someone who many turn to for comfort during hard times and for celebration in good ones. You are the ever-loving presence in their life. Or maybe you are the person people go to for guidance. They trust your wisdom and experience when it comes to planning, facing difficult choices and learning something new. You might think to yourself, "People say that I'm always the one who speaks up and defends them." It could be that you lean more toward a protective role.

Understanding your natural gifts and talents sharpens your discernment and helps you determine what type of support you might need and are best at giving. The Loving One might struggle with coddling themselves and look to the Guide to offer balance. In return, the Guide learns how to be more compassionate toward themselves and others.

To help you discover your builder type, go to theidentityresetbook.com/bookextras for a free, quick assessment quiz. You'll also receive additional information on how to strengthen your skill and the other types of Builders you might meet along the way.

How We Confuse Our Builders

In one of my grief groups a woman, who I'll call Donna, raised her hand and wanted to share something she'd been struggling with.

I invited her to share. "I tried talking to my mom when I was feeling sad. I expected her to be validating and comforting, but she just gave me tips on what to do. And it's not like what she said was bad—it was good. Just. . . not what I needed right then."

Group members nodded. One person said, "I know, right?" Followed by others who chimed in with, "They just don't get it." One man shook his head and exhaled, "These people are pointless after a loss."

I knew that feeling. That ache needs something *specific*: softness, warmth, to be held without being handed logic and lists. Sometimes you leave those moments angrier than before. Sometimes you wonder, *Why did I even open my mouth?*

But Donna mentioned a critical detail. She said she wanted validation and comfort but admitted her mom's suggestions was *good advice*. It just wasn't the kind that meets the soul when it's still breaking.

Donna had gone to the wrong person. She was aching for the Loving One, but had turned to her mother, a clear Guide. This isn't to say her mother didn't love her. Of course she did. But love comes in many forms. Sometimes what you need requires a different set of tools and a different kind of touch.

When I explained the Three Builders, I saw something click. Donna sat back and said, "That makes sense. My mom's amazing at helping me figure things out. If I'm ever in a jam, she's the first person I call. But emotional stuff? She tries, but it's not really her thing. I think I need to talk to my cousin instead."

A few weeks later, I asked how things were going. She told me it still hurts that her mother couldn't fully empathize with her, but she didn't take it personally anymore. She had started reaching out to her cousin instead—someone who didn't ask her to move on or clean up her pain. Just someone who sat with her in it. And when she needed a way to get through the day? Her mom still had the structure and strategy she could count on.

Grief still hurt. But the relationships around it felt a little less tangled, a little less sharp. Sometimes the shift isn't in changing the people around you. It's in recognizing what they can (and cannot) offer and allowing yourself to seek what you need from those who can actually give it.

Maybe, like Donna, you've been asking someone to give in ways they aren't yet equipped to give. That's not a you or them problem. It might not be a sign that you need to "cut them off" or fade away from the relationship either. It's simply a misalignment. Therefore, ask yourself: In this stage of my life, who am I encouraged to reposition? What type of relationships do I need to fill in the gaps?

Building Is a Pruning Process

Growing up, we had a grapevine in our backyard. Each summer, I'd watch my father cut the dead branches and the ones that were alive but not bearing fruit. This pruning process was necessary because empty branches draw energy and nutrients away from fruit-bearing ones.

The same principle applies to the relationships in your life. As you evaluate your inner circle, don't just honor those who have stayed—look for reciprocity. Like my father cutting back the barren branches, you may need to release connections that drain your energy and no longer nourish you. This might seem harsh, but mental, emotional, and energetic depletion comes at a cost. You are not required to sacrifice yourself at the expense of yourself. It's normal for building to look like letting go.

However, there will be times when you won't need to initiate the pruning at all. Some people will naturally drift, disengage, or step back on their own. While that can feel confusing—or even painful—it often becomes one of the most supportive parts of your after-loss journey. Life removes people to shield the parts of you they cannot hold. Therefore, know that not every ending counts as failure. The Builder in you protects what's becoming.

> *Pruning only feels like loss until the harvest comes.*

Cracks in the Foundation

Many of us struggle to let people in. We want their help. We want their comfort. But we fear what they might see if we come undone. Shame often stands between us and the support we need. It convinces us that we're either too much or not enough. It whispers lies like: *I deserved what happened; I'm not worthy of anything good; I'm too difficult to love; I can't seem to get anything right.* Contrary to what pop psychology tells us, shame isn't a feeling. If it were, it would come and go like other emotions. Shame is a belief, and it seeps into every part of our lives that touches it or gets too close. No wonder it makes us hide. If people don't see that I believe I'm bad, they'll keep me around and love and respect me.

That is a hard concept to contend with, because if I am the bad thing, how can I possibly receive or produce anything good? Yes, I released the shapeshifter, but how do I know this new version of me won't fail?

To understand why that fear runs so deep, consider this: If you give a child a crayon and say, "Please don't draw on the wall" and later they do—it makes sense to gently correct them. Maybe you take the crayon away and say, "We don't draw there." That child might feel a little guilty and think, *I did something I wasn't supposed to do*. But now imagine you yell, shame them, or react harshly by saying, "Why would you do that? You always mess things up! What's wrong with you?" Now it's no longer about the crayon. The child thinks: *Maybe something is wrong with me. Maybe I ruin everything.*

If the child internalizes that belief, it spills into other areas of their life. I see this often with people who tell me they felt abandoned as a child, whether physically because a parent wasn't present or emotionally if the parent *was* present but *not* emotionally attuned to them. Sometimes the child thinks to themselves, "Mom or dad wasn't there for me, so I must not be good enough." Or "Mom and dad divorced, so it must be my fault." Unfortunately, when parents don't take responsibility for their wounds, their children do.

Adults aren't exempt from this either. Shame doesn't care how many degrees you have, if you're sitting on a board, or are highly intelligent. It finds its way into the faces of women who laugh too brightly, into the pockets of men who grew up learning vulnerability is a weakness. We learn to pass it on like a family recipe. But shame is not medicine. It does not mend the spirit. It does not stitch the wound. It sends the pain underground: into silence, secrecy, and dark rooms where the heart loses its courage to be seen.

Shame is a universal struggle that, much like birth and death, touches everyone. We are taught to shame others. The thinking is, if I shame my child, they won't make that mistake. If I shame them for their mental health struggles, they will heal or act normal. If I shame them for their romantic relationship choices, they'll choose better.

Instead, it teaches the person with mental health struggles, "I can't talk about it." It tells people, "I have to hide my relationship problems." It says, "You can't talk about not having money, pretend instead"—and therefore, you never get help from those who can help you improve your situation. If you find yourself struggling to rely on the Three Builders, there might be a crack in your foundation, and shame is its name.

Mending happens when someone hears your story and holds it with care. This is where the Loving Builder steps in. They don't judge you for why you stayed, what you chose, or how you kept going and stopped. And that makes all the difference. Healing happens when we are introduced to experiences that contradict what trauma, pain, and loss made us accustomed to.[2] When someone responds differently than

[2] The Diary Of A CEO. "The Body Trauma Expert: This Eye Movement Trick Can Fix Your Trauma! The Body Keeps the Score!," December 23, 2024. https://www.youtube.com/watch?v=Qx5J5nwDBTo.

your shame expects, you finally feel the rupture begin to repair. It's the first proof that you are not what happened to you—and never were. That's how your True Identity starts to trust it's safe to be seen; it's also why community is important. *Builders don't shame the damage; they reinforce the foundation.* So, the next time shame shows up in your relationships, or in your decisions, try to name it, let someone see it, and allow yourself to be supported. With the right Builders beside you, the impossible becomes survivable, the survivable becomes bearable, and the bearable becomes growth.

Friendly Recap

Community is not about collecting more people; it's about positioning the right ones. The Protector, the Guide, and the Loving One are not luxuries—they are lifelines. They help us see what shame tried to hide, prune what trauma made heavy, and remind us that healing rarely happens in isolation. When you allow these Builders into your life, you begin to see that safety, wisdom, and love are not abstract hopes but tangible gifts available through relationships. Allow yourself to be protected when you are fragile, guided when you are unsure, and loved when you need reminding of who you are. Take the Builder's Quiz to get started on building your community: theidentityresetbook.com/bookextras.

Root Five

THE IDENTITY ROOT

This Is How We Heal

If everything that gave you a title, role, reputation, or wealth were gone—and you were simply you—how would you introduce yourself? Identity is not built on applause or approval. It is the steady flame no storm can extinguish, the treasure you carry into every season, and the presence you bring when all else is stripped away. It is the essence of who you are, the part no one can give you and no one can take away.

In the Releaser Root, we explored how identity can be like a treasure hidden away, guarded by a wounded dragon. Once the dragon is freed, you finally gain access to what was always yours. In the Builder Root, you learned how to use that treasure to shape your life—crafting rhythms, relationships, and ways of being that reflect who you are becoming.

Now, with the Identity Root, the work shifts again. It's not about accessing or constructing; it's about *embodying*—living from your core, day by day. This is where you carry your identity forward, not as something to protect behind walls, but as something to practice consistently and steward with care. To know your identity is to live in such a way that, even when roles change or losses come, you remain rooted in who you are.

What Is Essence?

Essence is the state of being before any action takes place. It is the "I am" beneath every "I do." It's that unwavering sense of self you carry in solitude, and the presence others feel before you ever introduce yourself. Essence is your original identity; it is your signature in the world.

There are four ways to recognize essence:

1. **It is unchanging.** Circumstances shift, but who you are endures.
2. **It is nontransactional.** Your identity exists apart from approval or reward.
3. **It is recognizable.** People often experience it as your unique energy, presence, or atmosphere.
4. **It is life-giving.** You feel most alive, and others feel safe with you.

Living from this place creates an inner sanctuary. It guides, supports, and grounds you. Being in alignment with your True Identity makes you consistent in character. You make decisions with clarity and confidence. This decreases impulsive harm—relationally, ethically, even financially—because your choices begin to align with your core values, not your fear or performance.

Identity Loss Creates Global Challenges

Many of the conflicts we see today, whether religious, political, or societal, are not just about differing opinions, they're about disoriented identities. When we don't know who we are, we're more likely to react from insecurity, ego, or inherited roles. And culture is quick to hand us stories of "us versus them," so we take refuge in groups that separate us. Nationalism, racism, gender wars, and modern-day tribalism all stem from this false identity built on division; it relies upon defining ourselves by who we are *not*, rather than who we can become together.

History is full of examples: the caste in India, apartheid in South Africa, and "manifest destiny" in the United States.

While Western culture teaches us, "I am what I own; I am what I consume," the Identity Root creates a radically different way of living: stewardship. Stewardship means taking loving responsibility for what has been entrusted to you: your story, your presence, your relationships, and the impact you have on others. When we understand who we are and take care of that person, we honor and cherish the life within others. Each person's true identity is seen as a treasure and gets to be celebrated.

The differences between us become those that are uniquely valued, not aspects to defend. Identity prides itself in its origins without weaponizing them. Stewardship calls us deeper than possession or achievement; it says, "I am responsible for what I hold," be it someone's heart, trust, vulnerability, or pain. That's because your true identity isn't only for you. It's a gift you carry for the benefit of everyone around you.

You can think of it this way: If your identity is the seed, your communities are the soil, and our world is the fruit. When the seed is wounded, its fruit will carry that ache. When the soil is harsh, even the healthiest seed can struggle to become all it's meant to be. And so, who we allow ourselves to evolve into after loss and transition touches everyone we encounter. However, this is to your benefit. It allows you to plant the legacy you longed for and to bring forth healing where survival once lived.

Identity Is Personal and Communal

The invitation of identity work is not just to name who you are, but to become that person—faithfully, imperfectly, day by day. This is the work of the final root: learning to live from your truth not occasionally, but consistently. You discover how to carry that truth forward through stewardship, not control.

However, becoming that person takes time. Identity work is slow work, and that process feels countercultural to the demands of hustle, speed, and performance. But lasting things don't grow quickly. From institutions like Disney, Amazon, and Ford to wonders like the Eiffel Tower and the pyramids, great and mighty structures take time to develop.

Healing, too, requires effort and slowness. It deepens when your identity is allowed to connect with others in safe, life-giving ways. In forests, scientists have discovered that when one tree begins to suffer, others nearby sense its need. Underground, fungal threads known as mycorrhizal networks connect the roots of different trees, enabling them to share nutrients like carbon and water with those that are struggling. Sometimes, this intricate web even passes along warnings of disease or danger. The forest survives because no root grows alone.

We are much the same. Our healing becomes possible not when we are isolated but when we are connected. Allow the Identity Root to connect to your other four roots and the lives of others. Give yourself permission to expand and be nourished in return. *Identity is sacred, slow, communal, and necessary for collective healing*. For every time you show up as your real self, and permit your true self to thrive among others, you become part of the invisible network that helps us all endure and flourish.

Chapter 12

The Practice of You

My mother never cooked with recipes. No measuring cups, no timers—only rhythm, instinct, and trust in her hands. She'd hum over a pot and laugh, calling herself the Master Chef like it was her birthright. That's how identity is made—by trusting that what rises within us is meant to be enjoyed and celebrated.

Yet, not all of us were raised in places that taught such trust. Some kitchens left us hungry, and others taught us we had to accept what we could. *You better eat what's in front of you.* We learned survival but never tenderness toward ourselves. The "Practice of You" is a personal invitation to reclaim what was missing in the kitchen: the chance to season your own life, choose your own portions, and what you want on your plate.

In culinary, the French phrase *mise en place* (pronounced *meez ahn plas*) means "to gather" or to have "everything in its place." Before a chef cooks, they prepare their station—every ingredient, every tool, is ready for what's to come. It's a practice that they take seriously, and it aids them in the process of showing up well. Therefore, The Identity Root helps you live out the contents of who you are.

Redeeming Values

For identity work, I focus on ***redeeming values*** instead of general values. A redeeming value is more than something you care about—it is a belief that both nourishes who you are becoming and rewrites the fear or wound beneath old emotional vows and trauma bargains. *While general values simply name what matters, redeeming values transform your relationship with them.* They take familiar areas of life—success, family, love, belonging—and give them new meaning in ways that heal and align with your true identity.

Below are examples of how a general value can be reframed into a redeeming value after loss, change, or transition:

Focus	**Value**	**Redeeming Value**
Provision	"I value being a provider."	"Providing is not only financial. My presence, care, and consistency are provisions, too."
Love	"I value love."	"Love does not require me to disappear, shrink, or betray myself. I am safe to be fully seen."
Leadership	"I value leadership."	"Leadership is not about control or proving myself—it is about serving from authenticity, not performance."
Belonging	"I value belonging."	"Belonging does not mean tolerating harm. I can belong without betraying myself to be accepted."
Family	"I value family."	"My role as a parent may change, but my identity remains. I am more than the roles I've held."

Trauma and life transitions change our lens of what we value and why. Redeeming values is an opportunity to attach a new, purposeful meaning to what's already important to you. Yet, alone, they are limited in impact. This brings us to the next section: how to turn those redeeming values into daily practices that shape your evolving identity.

Building Identity Actions

Every kitchen runs on more than recipes and tools. It runs on etiquette. Not the fancy kind, but the rules and rhythms that keep the space consistent. Chefs know that how you move in the kitchen is as important as what you cook. Your life works the same way. Therefore, we create **Identity Actions**—deeds you make to remain consistent with who you are.

Redeeming values tell you what matters. Identity Actions are how you live them out. Without action, values stay in the pantry—good in theory but never nourishing in practice. This is where your roots meet again. You might recall the concept of vows and bargains in the Shapeshifter Root:

The Emotional Vow says:
I got burned, so I'll never touch a hot stove again.

The Trauma Bargain says:
I'm going to stay out of the kitchen all together.

The Identity Root changes this. The Shapeshifter's survival vows get redeemed with identity actions. This is the reset:

> **The Redeeming Value:**
> *Safety is important to me, so I'll exercise caution.*
>
> **The Identity Action says:**
> *I'll use oven mitts and keep loose clothing away from the flames.*

Your Identity Actions are the small but steady rules you live by. They uphold your new self, help you stand tall in who you're becoming, and keep you disciplined when life feels precarious. Over time, they become the habits others respect you for because they shape how you treat people and how you treat yourself. You get to create new actions that support the person, the lifestyle, and the capacity of who you are now.

In Chapter Three, we met Franklin, who would not permit himself to take breaks. He felt the need to always be "on" or else "doing something" despite exhaustion. His emotional vow was: "Never again will I allow myself to go without." It was fortified with the trauma bargain of, "If I stay in motion, I won't have to face the discomfort underneath the stillness." In the Identity Root, that survival pattern resets:

> **The Redeeming Value:**
> *I honor rest as much as work.*
>
> **The Identity Action says:**
> *Each day, I allow my mind and body thirty minutes of true rest.*

Identity Actions generate real belief through practice, unlike traditional affirmations—which research demonstrates can backfire for those lacking confidence. For example, a landmark study found that people with low self-esteem felt worse after repeating positive statements, while those with high self-esteem saw improvements. These findings show affirmations are most effective for those who already believe them, not for those working to overcome doubt or rebuild trust in themselves.[1]

Based on years of working with clients rebuilding their identity, I developed the Identity Actions approach to address this gap. Instead of repeating what you hope to believe, we focus on embodying change through specific, repeated behaviors that reinforce your emerging self. Affirmations remind you of what you could become—if you believe them. Identity Actions ensure you become it by what you practice each day.

Your Identity Step

You've already started stocking your pantry with values. Now it's time to take it a step further. Earlier, in the Shapeshifter Root, you named your emotional vows and trauma bargains. Don't leave them sitting there. Bring them back into the kitchen. Take one of your vows and bargains and reset it here:

- Which redeeming value could strengthen you where that fear still lives?
- What Identity Action could reset the bargain into something life-giving?

---

[1] Koosis, Lisa A. (2024). "The Science of Affirmations: The Brain's Response to Positive Thinking," rev. by Dr. Brindusa Vanta, Ph.D., *MentalHealth.com*, June 25, 2024.

The Signature Dish: Who You Are

Somewhere along the way, your choices, mistakes, hopes, and tiny acts of courage simmer together into a flavor that's unmistakably yours. That's your signature dish. Every chef has one—some glorious, some peculiar, all honest. It's what people come back for, the thing they say, "If you want this, you have to go there." Your life deserves that same clarity. We create this by making a Signature Statement: one sentence that says, without apology, this is me. Think of it this way: When someone experiences your presence, what should linger? What do you want them to remember you by?

Too many of us, though, were never taught our own flavor. When life demands survival, you don't get much space to be playful or curious. You learn how to get food on the table, not how to make it memorable. That's why we start small in reclaiming what you want to be known for. A Signature Statement doesn't need to be polished, profound, or perfect. It isn't a slogan. It's simply your way of saying: *This is the dish I'm finally choosing to make mine.*

One Ingredient:
"I may not know my full recipe yet, but I want to season life with kindness."

One Person:
"For now, I want to be the safe place my kids can come to."

One Act:
"I don't have a big vision, but I feel better when I write in my journal each morning."

For a season, I worked in the death care department of a life insurance company. When members died without a listed beneficiary—or when their beneficiary died—it became my job to find one. I combed through hundreds of obituaries and files, hoping to trace a thread to the next of kin who could claim the insurance money. After reading obituary after obituary, I started asking myself the existential question, *Who do I want to be?* For me, my Signature Statement comes down to three things:

- to bring peace with my presence,
- to help people feel seen,
- to restore people to their true selves.

Whether with a client, in another workspace, on vacation, or among those I love—I ask myself, *how can I be more of myself around them?* It's no coincidence that people walk away calmer, more themselves, and a little closer to their internal truth after our time together.

We can't control who people say we are. However, we can influence it. We influence people to see us as funny by consistently landing the punch line. We influence them to view us as insightful by offering wisdom or sound advice. We influence others to call us good by living with integrity.

Legacy isn't accidental; it's built choice by choice, day by day. And in the end, your signature isn't what you hoped to be. It's who you practiced becoming.

Your Identity Step

What gives you life when you offer it to others? Name and write down one or two things. Those are your signatures.

Hosting: How You Show Up

Your signature dish is what you offer the world; hosting is how people experience it. What type of environment do you create for connection, collaboration, and belonging when you're with people? The answer matters. Being a master chef extends further than the dish on the plate; it includes the experience you create around the table.

Your identity works the same way. It's great that you're showing up as yourself. Just as a restaurant thinks about lighting, sound, scent, and decor to create a memorable dining experience, you can design the cues that shape how people experience *you*. This isn't about being performative—it's how your presence communicates safety, belonging, and respect. It's the opportunity for your identity actions and your signature statement to come alive. Hosting is where all your culinary skills show up. It's when *what you know* becomes *what you show*. Now, let's begin with your identity hosting:

- **Environment (decor):** Restaurants pay attention to details: colors, furniture, arrangement. In your life, this looks like your personal presentation. How you present yourself—your posture, your presence, your space—sets the tone for how people read you. Does the world you create on the outside match the truth you're building on the inside?
- **Boundaries (cleanliness):** Clean spaces steady the mind; boundaries steady the heart. They're an identity action: practical ways you show respect for yourself and others, keeping resentment from piling up like dirty dishes.
- **Service (hospitality):** Great restaurants know service is everything. Service is the way your presence meets the room. It shows in how you listen, how you regard others, and how you make space for them without erasing yourself. This is where your signature dish becomes lived: through gestures that say "I see you," not "I'm performing for you." The goal isn't charm or effort; it's sincerity that lands.

- **Consistency (menu):** A menu tells you what to expect. People feel secure when your words, actions, and values align. What you season your life with becomes the steady flavor people trust.
- **Tone (lighting):** Your tone can light a room or dim it. The way you speak—gentle, warm, or sharp—sets the atmosphere before anything else does. Think of it as the lighting that lets your signature dish be seen clearly.

Your Identity Step

Take a moment to design your restaurant—your identity—on purpose. Picture yourself setting a table people can rely on. Then walk through the five cues: environment, boundaries, service, consistency, and tone. Most of us rarely stop to examine how we're showing up; we move through the day on instinct. A little reflection strengthens safety, belonging, and trust. Identify one area that needs more attention, choose one small practice you can repeat for the next seven days and keep it somewhere you'll see it.

Repairing the Table

The best kitchens have bad nights. A dish comes out cold. A server makes a mistake. The customer complains. When that happens, the manager doesn't shrug and say, "Well, too bad." They find a way to repair the experience either by remaking the dish, offering a discount, or allowing the person to be heard. The goal is restoring harmony between the table and the host.

Life mirrors this. No matter how faithfully you practice your identity actions, or how clear your Signature Statement is, there will be moments when harm enters the room. Sometimes it's a misunderstanding with a friend, a disagreement with someone you respect, or your family that creates the tension. Repairing the table is not about pretending the harm never happened. It's about being honest. Just as a manager assesses the situation to decide the best course of action in the kitchen, we too must assess the state of our relationship before rebuilding.

Three Questions to Ask Before Repairing a Relationship

1. Is this relationship safe enough to approach again?
2. Am I grounded enough—mind and body—to enter the conversation?
3. Is the other person willing to work toward harmony?

Receiving a definitive yes to each of those questions is the minimum requirement for repair. When those answers finally align, repair becomes possible. Possible doesn't mean easy or guaranteed. It doesn't promise the relationship will return to what it was—because it won't. It may grow, change, or become something unexpected, but it will not go back.

Forgiveness and repair are not acts of revision. They don't rewrite the harm. They name it with clarity, set boundaries with strength, and create the space where most of your roots intertwine: the Truth Seeker to see what happened, the Releaser to let go, the Builder for remodeling, and Identity to anchor you. Sometimes, part of that work is accepting the grief of what happened so you can receive whatever comes next.

Children are often rushed into premature forgiveness. I sat in Central Park in New York City and watched two siblings fight over a jar of bubbles. The brother who wanted the bubbles pushed his sister to the ground. Their father got up immediately and said, "That's your family, say sorry!" The boy mumbled an "I'm sorry," and the sister, still holding the jar of bubbles, was told to say, "I forgive you." She did, and handed over the jar, even though her face said she wasn't ready. The cycle of forgiveness was complete—or so it seemed.

I am confident the father meant well. He wanted harmony, for the tension to dissolve quickly. His actions were driven by love, but he missed the deeper point of repair. It's not enough to say, "I'm sorry" or "I forgive you." Forgiveness isn't a transaction, words we say and move on from. Some foods need to simmer before being served, and the process is delicate. Repair takes intentional effort, transparency, and readiness. Just as the master chef listens to their guests' frustrations, we, too, must face the hurt before we can restore our comfort.

I discovered this through my healing journey. As I sought to fortify my identity, I had enormous feelings of anger and grief. I was angry at what my parents did and grieving what I never received. I was angered by the way I had let former friends treat me and grieved in knowing they found their actions permissible. More than anything, I was frustrated with how I treated myself. My work has proven I'm not alone in this. There are many people who hold both grief and anger, frustration and disappointment toward family and friends.

However, as I transitioned through my roots, it was important for me to let go of certain relationships and make a faithful attempt to repair and build others. Two of them were the connections with my parents. It took years of expressing how I felt (which risked vulnerability for me), not growing defensive with their responses (whether they were or not), and allowing myself to see both their humanity *and* my own misunderstandings.

They had never parented a child like me, in the situations they were in, at the ages that they were, in the world I grew up in—all while fighting battles they never wanted me to encounter. Strangely enough, the more compassion I learned to extend toward myself—accepting the places where I had been both villain and victim—the more I could forgive the villain in others and hold love for the heart they shared with me.

Healing, for me, looked like accepting that the version of them I desired might never come. Each of us have our limitations, but healing also meant building a relationship with who they are today and finding ways to remain in harmony. Today, as an adult, I hold two truths: They were doing their best, and their best still left wounds I had to heal. I can resolve what's possible between us without neglecting or abandoning the person I've become.

While I don't believe repair is possible with everyone, including some parents, establishing peace with those who make it possible might be a worthy aim. A master chef won't find praise among every guest they host and neither will you. Chefs learn to dismantle conflict when they can, compromise when it makes sense to, and walk away knowing they didn't forsake who they are for the appeasement of others.

Friendly Recap

1. **Principles shape identity.** They're the ingredients that flavor everything you create.
2. **Actions prove identity.** They redeem old vows and bargains by showing who you are through what you consistently do.
3. **Identity leaves an experience.** The way you host shapes how people remember you and how you think of yourself.

Chapter 13

Stewardship

"10,000 people?"

I stared at the computer screen and started to panic.

What am I going to do?

This is too much.

My organization, Learning About Grief, had reached almost 10,000 followers on social media. Looking back, this feels small, but it was a big deal to me then. There were people on the waitlist for my grief groups, and I was receiving plenty of inquiries-turned-clients for my one-to-one sessions. I called my good friend, Ruby, who was a consistent source of comfort and encouragement.

"CONGRATULATIONS, MY SISTER! THAT'S GREAT NEWS! WOOOO! GO, ASHLEY, GO!" Ruby screamed over the phone. She was the perfect hype woman, a go-to motivator, and when she was happy for you, the whole world knew.

But I wasn't excited. Thankful, sure, but I wasn't thrilled.

"Your hard work is paying off, Ash." She said.

"Yeah, but could you imagine 10,000 people in a room with us? That's a lot of people. I'm responsible for these thousands, and that doesn't include my clients."

We eventually hung up, and while people were praising me, I was nervous. I planned how I could shut down Learning About Grief or at least slow it down. I didn't want thousands of followers to talk to—I wanted out.

Years of being in leadership roles and working directly under executives, presidents, and company owners taught me one thing: to whom much is given, much is required. I felt emotionally arrested by the weight of lives I had stewardship over. Leadership isn't confined to going first and calling the shots; it's about learning how to be the biggest servant, the one who holds the highest level of accountability and responsibility. You are the go-to person for putting out constant "fires" when life goes wrong.

I didn't have 10,000 followers. I had 10,000 names, faces, and hearts who were impacted by grief, loss, and hardship. My identity wasn't only for me anymore—it was for everyone else whom it would influence and impact. I stared at the waiting list and the numbers with questions: *What will I do with what I've been entrusted? What am I stewarding?*

Root Vegetables and Hidden Growth

Everyone kept telling me how quickly my audience had grown—how remarkable it was for someone who had endured widowhood twice to reach that many people, that fast. But nothing about it felt quick to me. What others named as "progress" felt more like a long, slow crawl through grief, decisions, and the hope that whatever I offered might land gently in someone else's heart. It may have looked sudden from the outside, but only because most of my becoming happened underground.

Root vegetables like carrots, beets, and potatoes are hidden cultivars whose most vital growth occurs underground, out of sight, and out of immediate recognition. Unlike fruits or leafy greens, root veggies *require darkness* to develop fully. If exposed to light, some—like potatoes—become toxic, turning green and developing solanine, which is poisonous. In the same way, some of your own most important growth happens "in the dark," away from public view. Exposure too soon can be harmful, not helpful. It is a gift to fortify your identity in the hidden seasons of your life.

Root vegetables also have a resilience that goes unnoticed by most. They survive and thrive because they know how to endure changing environments. They draw from the deep, rich nutrients in the soil, storing up resources to endure droughts and harsh conditions. In the garden, their strength isn't showy, but it is essential.

What does this have to do with your identity? For root-identity growers, stewardship is an invitation to grow your capacity for empathy, wisdom, and resilience—the qualities that sustain you through life's "winters." These characteristics are not visible in the way wealth or status might be, but they are no less valuable. In fact, they may be the very qualities that allow you to weather seasons others wouldn't survive.

- *For the CEO* whose company is in transition, the next chapter is built in long, sleepless nights and quiet boardrooms—growth that outsiders can't see.
- *For the empty nester,* discovering self happens in the privacy of an echoing house, where the work of grief, reinvention, and reclaiming purpose unfolds.

- *For the grieving person,* healing takes root beneath the surface, in silent tears and ordinary routines that no one applauds.
- *For those navigating singleness or post-divorce*, the reset happens in solitude, where you learn to trust your own company and learn who you are outside of a relationship.
- *For new parents,* the world sees a birth announcement, but the hard work is done in midnight feedings, an emergency doctor visit, and the private anxieties of becoming someone's safe place.

Your hidden work isn't wasted. Like a carrot pushing through hard soil, you're making the ground softer for those who will follow. Stewardship is about honoring this unseen growth without the promise of an audience.

It Wasn't Always This Good

Many want the fruit; few are willing to endure the dark to grow it. My in-between years were not glossy, linear, or triumphant. Nothing about cultivating who I am now felt beautiful or "inspirational." For example, my path entailed:

- Surviving childhood fractures while trying to love the people who caused them
- Losing the man I loved and every version of my life attached to him
- Burying three family members six months later
- Leaving a great job, to relocate to one that laid me off after two weeks
- Piecing together income, identity, and dignity at the same time
- Trying to build a business while barely holding myself together

- Watching it crumble because grief took all the strength I had
- Falling in love again, daring to imagine a future
- Becoming widowed again
- Collapsing under the weight of it
- Grieving the grandmother whose voice comforted my own
- Rebuilding myself from dust, questions, and stubborn hope
- Outlining a book I wasn't sure I was "ready" to do
- Pausing that book when my family fractured
- Enduring bouts of sadness and mental fatigue
- Returning to my work with more honesty than perfection
- Growing Learning About Grief from compassion, not strategy
- Discovering the strength and softness of my true identity
- Being praised for the healed version of me no one saw being sewn together
- And sitting here, writing the book you're holding now

Before success, there is survival.
Before applause, there is loss.
Before healing is visible, it is lived, raw and unglamorous.

Yes, there were many moments of highs, lows, and stability in between these moments. From the outside, most people only saw the harvest and the rough patches. They missed the internal battles I faced—the doubts, insecurities, internal compromises, and quiet celebrations in moments society deemed unmeasurable.

Yet, somehow, my identity remained intact. In your emptiness, you can know who you are and have peace with that person. That will make you able to evolve and grow not only who you are, but what you're doing, because of what's inside you.

How to Steward Identity from Below

Stewarding your identity in the "root" season isn't glamorous. It's not loud, and it's rarely visible. Here's how to uphold who you are:

- **Embrace the silence:** Silence is not confined to the absence of noise and people. It's the presence of unclaimed space. People fear silence because it threatens their sense of momentum or worth and causes reflection. But silence is the rehearsal room where you tune your instrument before anyone else hears you play. It's where you catch the off-notes and harmonics of your own identity, without external noise setting your tempo.

  Practice: Sit in silence for five minutes, then jot down the first "background noise" thought that surfaces. Is it truly your voice, or an echo from somewhere else? What does your mind and body cling to?
- **Redirect your resources:** In the dark, when external feedback is minimal, use your resources to become innovative. Resilience is an adaptive intelligence. In this space, you have permission to challenge dominant cultural and societal rules without fear. This builds ethical courage—your ability to break molds and stay true to who you are when external praise isn't given.

  Practice: Do an "inventory walk" through your story—spot three skills or traits you picked up in struggle that don't look impressive but are rare in others. How could you replant them in this season? Stewardship is using what the world deems "leftovers" as your main ingredients.
- **Steward your time:** Explore which interruptions are invitations and which are distractions.

Sometimes, the richest parts of your becoming grow inside what feels like a detour.

These interruptions become unexpected pollinators. Other moments are distracting and lack enrichment. Begin noticing detours. This will help you discern what's truly calling for your presence versus what's pulling at your attention.

Practice: For one week, keep a simple "interruption log." Notice when your plans get derailed—by a person, a distraction, a delay, or a lack of energy. Then ask:

- What is this moment revealing about who I am under pressure?
- Is there something I'm being invited to notice, feel, or reconsider?
- If I could treat this interruption as a teacher, what might it show me about my real priorities or unclaimed desires?

Stewardship from Above

Aboveground plants and fruits—like tomatoes and apples—announce their growth to the world. Their progress is obvious, but it comes with a price: exposure, vulnerability, and the constant need for protection and pruning. Visibility brings its own set of risks. You need strong, healthy boundaries, intentional replenishment, and safeguards against burnout. We learn to appreciate those seasons spent underground because they let us grow roots deep enough to survive the spotlight. When you finally surface, you need more than ambition—you need grounding.

When I first started college, I thought I wanted to be a TV journalist. In my broadcasting class, a fellow student said, "When I graduate, I want to be on CNN!"

Our professor shook his head: "No, when you graduate, start at a small-town news station."

We all wondered why he had such low expectations. He explained, "You're new. You're going to make mistakes. You don't want to make rookie errors on global television. Make them where few are watching. Then, when you're ready for the limelight, you're not only visible—you're prepared."

Honor the sunlight you have access to. In your above-ground season, the Identity Root asks: How will you tend to what's been revealed? In the last chapter, hosting was about making space for others' needs and comfort—setting the table, tending the atmosphere, welcoming their stories. Here, above ground, the focus shifts: *How do you steward your own presence when your story is in the open?* The spotlight doesn't just reveal what you want people to see—it exposes what you need to work on.

That's not a weakness; that's an opportunity. Above ground, stewardship is about using your visibility as a mirror and a megaphone: to keep yourself honest, to serve others, and to prove that real growth is built in daylight and the shadows. This is where your roots work in tandem. The Truth Seeker Root exposes where you're still performing as the Shapeshifter, and also where greater discernment is required. The Releaser Root enables you to shed what's no longer needed—be it opinions, habits, or mindsets. The Builder Root teaches you how to receive feedback and use your Identity Voice to give it.

- *For the CEO* in the spotlight, it means using influence to build up others, mentor, or champion change. This builds your legacy and mission.
- *For the parent,* it means modeling vulnerability, asking for support, and creating a safe, nurturing environment where growth is possible.
- *For the creative or leader,* it's stewarding your platform whether that's through educating, inspiring, or leading important social change.

- *For those in community,* it's encouraging others and meeting them where they are with support and encouragement. Allow yourself to serve and be compassionate and understanding.
- *For the griever,* it means protecting your journey through loss. It might look like giving yourself permission to say no to events, to rest when needed, or to ask for compassion instead of pretending you're "okay."

You cultivate honesty in the way you move through public spaces, teaching others that true stewardship of who you are means honoring your limits and letting yourself consistently show up as yourself.

How to Steward Identity from Above

Attention expands the room you stand in and the expectations inside it. Here's how to stay grounded in who you are:

- **Seek true replenishment.** Sunshine seems great until you realize too much of it burns you. While being underground shows you how to cultivate silence, and might require you to become intentional about interacting with others, being visible requires willful solitude. Now that you have identity, and it's celebrated by others, you need to ensure you do not lose it to others' demands. Block off time to reset your vision or reevaluate personal goals. This recalibrates you for greater productivity and long-term success.

  Practice: Schedule a deliberate off-stage moment. Block off personal time on your calendar in the same way you allocate time for a meeting or a doctor's visit. What gets scheduled gets done. Where do you feel most drained right now? What would true replenishment look like?

- **Be cautious of comparison.** The sun shines differently on everyone depending upon the season and time of day. Keep in mind that some plants require more light to thrive than others do. What fuels one plant will destroy another. Take joy in the season of growth you are in now. In the words of author Jon Acuff, "Don't compare your beginning to someone else's middle."[1]

  Practice: Create an "Already Bloomed" list. List everything you've accomplished or learned this year (including small wins or quiet changes)—especially things you did in your own timing. When you're tempted to compare, reread this list and remind yourself that your journey is not a competition; it's a garden. You are not competing to exist in your own life. In the garden, your presence beautifies what's present.

The Garden Is Bigger Than You

There comes a moment when you stand in your garden, see the fruit, and understand this wasn't planted for one table. What hangs on your branch isn't a reward for effort; it's an invitation. The harvest says, feed the world around you. Root deep, but notice how much depends on what you share.

This world tells you to build fences, stack trophies, and name yourself the hero. But the truth is simpler: Abundance rises from a shared field. Growth is a chorus, not a solo. Interdependence strengthens the trunks that stand through every season, delivering water where thirst lives. Community is not the backup plan; it's the architecture of every future worth planting.

[1] Acuff, J. (2017). *Finish: Give Yourself the Gift of Done*. Penguin.

Sometimes the garden forgets its softness. Weeds climb, gates rust shut, fruit spoils when guarded by fear. The labor feels uneven in the heat of it all. Scarcity whispers, "Hoard what you grow." True stewardship asks for the courage to offer, to restore, to reach across the rows. It celebrates power *within,* and power *to,* and power *shared*—not dominance over. Stewardship leads by listening. It looks beyond a single patch of land, studies the soil, notices who is without water, who has not known the sweetness of the harvest. In the end, leadership is a sacred tending: It calls forth what is good, and opens the gate for connection and presence.

"It takes a village to raise a child"—yes. It also takes a village to raise a vision, to nurture hope, to carry sorrow home.

Who eats from what you've grown? Does the fruit reach hungry mouths or circle back to your own hand? When you see ground that's been neglected, what do you offer—labor, seeds, a voice to break up stone? Whose life have you witnessed?

The steward notices every life entwined—plant, neighbor, stranger, child—and holds the responsibility to lift all. In the interplay of roots and fruit, solitude and gathering, each act of stewardship shapes the world we share. No identity flourishes in isolation. Be the one who tends the whole garden. Cultivate a legacy that outlives your own harvest. We flourish together, or we wither the same way the garden does.

Growth is proven not in how much you can gather for yourself, but in how freely you can share what your life has produced.

Fruit that is locked away spoils; it breeds bitterness, loneliness, and pain where joy was meant to be experienced.

When you practice true stewardship, your gifts don't stop at your own table. They ripple out—nourishing families, strengthening organizations, reshaping communities, and, in small but unmistakable ways, shifting culture. The fruit of your healing, your wisdom, and your love, can sweeten boardrooms, soften the hard corners of family legacies, and seed hope across neighborhoods and nations.

Examples of Identity Stewardship in Roles

- **The Teacher:**
  You notice the student who always sits at the back, call their name, invite their questions, and make space for their voice. Wisdom multiplies when you sow confidence and curiosity in others, never when you hoard knowledge in arrogance.
- **The Hairdresser or Barber:**
  You do more than cut and style. Your chair is a confessional, your hands are an act of care. You listen without judgment, celebrate every small triumph, and hold space for transformation that goes deeper than appearances. Stewardship here is in the stories remembered and the confidence built. You remind us that beauty appears when someone feels safe enough to be themselves.
- **The Corporate Mentor:**
  You don't just mentor—you make room. You spot potential early, speak someone's name in the rooms they can't yet reach, and clear paths they didn't know existed. In your hands, legacy is measured by who rises because you did, and who widened their capacity because you believed in it.

- **The Influencer:**
  You resist the temptation to be the loudest in the room, instead asking, "Who isn't being heard?" and use your influence to make the table longer, not just the stage higher.
- **The Father:**
  Your role isn't only about providing, but about presence—reading the bedtime story, teaching patience at the dinner table, listening when it's easier to fix. You know that fatherhood is a garden of gestures: tying shoes, wiping tears, and showing what love looks like in how you treat your children's mother, their siblings, and yourself. You plant seeds of safety and identity every day.

Stewarding who you are allows you to be a better steward of people, places, and opportunities. You show up in the world having peace with who you are and acceptance of who others are and choose to be without disturbing the world within you.

Stewardship and Identity Bring Peace

Many of us go to places to find peace, but what is it like to experience it when the child is sick, the divorce papers are served or signed, the casket is laid in the ground, the diagnosis is given? Peace is not just the absence of chaos, it's what we have in spite of it.

Peace is Anne Frank writing under Jewish persecution, "In spite of everything, I still believe that people are really good at heart. I don't think of all the misery, but of the beauty that still remains."[2] It was the enslaved Black Americans who

[2] Frank, Anne. *Anne Frank: The Diary of a Young Girl*, 1973.

sang melodies of freedom while being bound to a field. Peace shows up when the CEO isn't sure if he'll make payroll or has to undergo a major crisis or pivot. It is the deep inner knowing when your child goes off to college, or when the retirement fund you built runs low.

Perhaps the greatest gift of the Identity Root is everlasting peace. Calmness depends on circumstance and environment; peace depends upon the person who wishes to carry it. As Black Elk, an Indigenous American Medicine Man said, "The first peace. . .is that which comes within the souls of people when they realize their relationship, their oneness with the universe and all its powers, and when they realize at the center of the universe dwells the Great Spirit, and that its center is. . .within each of us."[3]

Peace extends beyond emotional calm. It's neither found in the absence of noise, tension, or grief nor dependent on your mood. That's why it confuses people.

Peace is presence.
Peace is alignment.
Peace is knowing who you are when the world says differently.
Peace is trust—not control.

Peace is what arrives when your soul stops searching for an exit. It settles in, pays attention, and chooses to live within the life you already have. It takes up residence when you can look at your identity with love and acceptance—knowing that acceptance doesn't mean liking every circumstance, only trusting that none of it diminishes the power within you.

---

[3] Marken, J.W., Deloria, V., and Neihardt, J.G. (1979). Black Elk speaks: being the life story of a holy man of the Oglala Sioux as Told Through John G. Neihardt. *The American Indian Quarterly* 5 (3): 254. doi: 10.2307/1183527.

Peace lets you see who you are and call it enough, in both your imperfections and your strength. It shows up as:

- **Ease.** You don't have to manage the room. You can just *be*.
- **Alignment.** Your internal world matches the environment you create externally.
- **Safety.** The felt sense of being protected and held.
- **Belonging.** Finding home within yourself, including in the presence of others.

You don't have to filter yourself to maintain the balance. You can release the responsibility of carrying everything, for everyone, everywhere, always. Identity is the unshakeable center of who you are—the deep-down story you tell yourself about your worth, your purpose, and your place in the world. For many people, peace feels fragile because it's tied to things that can change: a job, a relationship, an achievement, the approval of others. When those things shift, that sense of peace disappears. If your sense of self is built on unstable ground—external wins, constant productivity, always being "good" or needed—then every setback or criticism can shake you.

But when your identity is grounded in something deeper—your inherent dignity and personhood—peace becomes less about managing circumstances and more about inhabiting your life. This kind of peace isn't about "achieving" a feeling but instead settling into yourself. It doesn't come from controlling every outcome or shapeshifting for superficial wins and temporary acceptance. It comes from knowing you're enough, even when life is messy, uncertain, or unfair.

Identity answers the question, "Who am I when everything else is stripped away? And who will I become should I gain it all back?" Its root, in all its loving power, gives you the confidence and joy to be that person. The one you discover within doesn't have to be perfect. You only need to be you.

Stay rooted in yourself. Breathe into the life you *already* carry. The work is not to escape, but to return—again and again—to who you are, and call it enough. May your identity give you the courage to stay, and the peace to call yourself home. This is the identity reset.

To Become, We Must Reset

i have seen what it looks like
to build a house
to replant a tree
to open the door to a room that used to
  be broken
and see it made new.

people stop and say,
look at what you've done.
they see it.
they understand it.
they applaud.

but when you begin to rebuild
yourself—
the walls no one can see,
the voice you used to swallow,

the boundaries you are only now
beginning to hold—

no one claps.

there are no time-lapse videos
of you learning how to stay when you
used to run.
there are no congratulatory dinners
for finally speaking truth
without apologizing for how it lands.

the grief that had no funeral
now sits beside the growth that has no
name.

you become a little quieter.
a little clearer.
a little harder to manipulate.

and they say,
you've changed.
you're acting strange.
what's up with you now?

but they are not asking about your pain.
they are asking for the version of you
they could predict.

they remember the one who said yes
when you meant no.
the one who kept the peace,
even when it cost you
the softest parts of yourself.

and this new version—
this one who pauses before offering,

who doesn't explain every move,
who no longer shrinks to fit—
is unfamiliar.

they haven't met you
since the undoing.

your patterns have not yet become habits.
your voice has not yet settled into ease.
and so they ask, without asking,
will you go back to what made us feel safe?

but this is not about them.

this is about how you stay.
how you keep holding your shape
when their discomfort grows louder
than your old fear.

it's not that they don't want you to be
whole.
they just don't recognize
what healing looks like
when it stops asking for permission.

and if they are not happy with who you are
becoming—
let that be their burden to carry.

you are not here
to shapeshift again.

you are the one
who has survived the burning,
and is now learning how to build
without smoke in your lungs.

so let them adjust.
or let them leave.

but vow to me this: *never again* will you
leave yourself to make others
feel less alone
in your becoming.

Index